D0885109

So, You're The Manager...
Now What?

Kurt Reinhart

© 2010 Kurt Reinhart. All rights reserved. Printed in the United States of America. All rights reserved. No part of this book my be reproduced or transmitted in any form or by any means, electronic or mechanical, including photocopying, recording, or by an information storage and retrieval system without permission in writing from the author, except by a reviewer, who may quote brief passages in a review. Published by Kurt Reinhart. First Edition

Although the author and publisher have made every effort to ensure the accuracy and completeness of information contained in this book, we assume no responsibility for errors, inaccuracies, omissions, or any inconsistency herein. Any slights of people, places, or organizations are unintentional.

Cover and interior design by Alex LaFasto

ISBN 978-0-9825672-1-0

To my wife and children
thank you for your love.

To Jackie F.
thank you for the opportunities to be a
teacher of managers.

To Alex L.
thank you for helping to shape my line of sight.

Contents

Acknowledgements

Having completed my first book, I have to wonder how much has changed considering that acknowledgement. They are the same people for the same reasons. So what to do? As an improvisational response, I could say "ditto". That would be rude. As a means to accomplish a necessary goal of acknowledging the insight, direction, experience and growth, I will say thank you to all. They are too many to mention and too many to contemplate.

Perhaps the better way to acknowledge others is to provide a context for the book itself. At the start of my training workshops, I will always offer the answers to three questions: why, what and who. The idea is based on the notion some attendees did not have a say in the decision to be at the workshop. Therefore having been told to show up, they may not have the faintest clue as to "why we are here, what will happen and who is facilitating this whole thing". I will share the answers as they pertain to this book.

This book's reason for being or the "why" question is there may very well be young team members moving into positions of management without the helpful insight and context necessary to lead others effectively. They are certainly able to lead. It is more an issue of not near enough practice in getting things done through others. It may immediately appear I am writing this book for new managers only. This book can be reviewed with many readers in mind. For instance, the tactics and approaches can easily educate or reinforce managers who have been doing it for a while. Furthermore, it may assist with your friends and family relationships. Having had tremendous experiences in the field, my desire is to provide insight to whoever is willing to learn more about their skills, abilities and knowledge.

The format for this book, or the "what," is designed to provide a balance of learning for the reader. It will include review of context and definition regarding the topic of the chapter. It will explore tactics and tips provided for immediate practice. It will also encourage ongoing learning and adoption. This format is based on the perspective I have gained from working with a variety of organizations, multiple industries and all levels of team members who make it happen everyday. It allows me to compile and share best practices in effective management.

The potentially big question is "who" are you? I could list my professional experiences of over 20 plus years within retail, wholesale, telecom, hospitality and manufacturing industries. There is the variety of key roles including sales, account management, buying, media production, merchandising and training. I could state simply "I read a lot." Ultimately, I will rest my credentials on having been blessed to work with some awesome people in large to small organizations in North America and Europe. I have gained as much as I have given. I paid attention and still do. Lastly, I believe in the mindset that there is always something new to learn, even in the most unlikely of places.

Intro

(or your part in the book)

There are so many aspects to discuss in management. In fact, too many. This book and its chapters will take you on a journey to a desired destination. The journey may be filled with challenges, while others may simply be fun. This book is designed to give you insight into what may occur regarding some of the most common (and perhaps uncommon) managerial situations.

Consider this:

You have been a team member with an organization for one year. This organization has been going through great change from rapid growth, a change in senior management and an aggressive approach to getting back market share. At your current location, your manager has been promoted to take on bigger management responsibilities. Due to this fast track and some subtle mentoring, you have been selected to be the new manager at your location. The team of eight was your peer one day and now you are their leader the next. What will they be thinking or feeling? What is the best approach tactically to establish your position, vision and, ultimately, your credibility as leader?

This scenario (battle) is real for managers. Questions like "what do I do?", "what will I say?" and "what if this happens?" are all valid. While this book shares insight into what matters to a manager and what makes the most sense to get things done. There are no absolutes. Two things will factor, the context and your perspective. My first book *What If?* tackled the formulaic approach to management. The only formula is A (the defined expectation within the job) + Variables (the unknown context surrounding the expectation) = Customized Approach (the improvisational reaction to meet the expectation based on your perspective).

There are four sections designed to explore your realities within the job. Each section will have chapters to go deeper into those realities. Section one deals with the foundational skills in managing others. It is the "you-side" of the equation and what you need to be successful. The next section looks at the business. It may raise the most questions. Please note, I cannot answer many of those questions. It has been my experience these questions typically have to do with the specific "what if's" in the business or specific operational aspect of the job. The information provided in this text is only secondary to the expectations of the company. The idea is to provide as much of a wide birth as possible so as to ensure a general overview. Section three dives into how these core skills begin to take shape when working with and through others. The direction will change from a singular lens to that of a team lens. The last section will look at how choice factors into the manager job, especially those which may be the most challenging. It is no mistake the first three sections create a foundation. The end will be how to apply that foundation to the decisions which will affect you, your business and your team.

Each chapter will look at how an awareness and understanding of a managerial topic can influence how you accomplish your goals and the growth of others. Each chapter matters to your job within a relative context. You pick your wins. Each chapter will also share individual activities, as well as action plans to promote adoption within a topic. The accountability of action lies with you.

Now as you journey in this book, it may leave you wanting more. While each chapter will explore best practices for immediate practice and adoption, your responsibility will be to look beyond these ideas. They only represent my perspective within a literary construct. While I have a library of information to share with my clients, this is only a book. It does not allow for the details in a more specific context. If you have more questions, seek me or others out to gain the answers to those types of questions. Let this book represent just one facet of all of your research into management.

Thank you and please enjoy the book.

Part 1: YOU

Let's not complicate our relationship by trying
to communicate with each other.
                                        - Ashleigh Brilliant

1

Communication

Communication exists in all things. Therefore, this will be a big chapter. This is an incredibly broad reaching and general topic. The goal is to provide insight into the interaction between people, implying both verbal and non-verbal realities in a relational context. It is about interpersonal communication; particularly as it applies to a manager-team member relationship. Since it is impossible to not do this in every aspect of your job, communication will be discussed in many ways throughout this book.

Within our very recent history, technology has changed how we communicate. Speed and convenience has replaced the art of talking. We are losing our practice in just talking to each other. With the very recent advent of the PDA, smart phones and internet on the go, we are relying on devices for efficiency sake. Then we wonder "how we ever got along without our Blackberry?" Simple, we talked to each other. It may be looked at as inefficient by the current standards of day, however it does work.

What is communication? Is it a process? A process is cold and calculative. It implies a beginning, middle and end. An argument could be made that communication does have those very same elements: speak, hear, distill, repeat process. Although I agree someone speaks and someone hears. This back and forth approach systemically implies a process. I prefer to define communication as a relationship. This applies a much bigger and more engaging experience with much more at stake. You have to take a more active stand within the exchange. Consequently, you have more to risk and more to gain as a result of being more involved. It is a mind-set shift. And it involves much more work.

The quality of the communication is also at question. When communicating with another person, a perception and understanding of the communication is being internalized. Does the sender understand the best way to reach the receiver? And does the receiver have the same basis of understanding as the sender. All too often, the mere speaking of words is not sufficient. There are three factors being taken into account by the receiver within the exchange: words (verbalization), tone (vocalization) and body language (visualization). There are varying degrees of importance placed on each of these factors. If you research communication, you will discover a range of importance by percentages applied within the action of communication. Typically, a higher percentage of any exchange between parties is weighted towards the unspoken communication, body language. The least percentage rests with the actual words being spoken. If that is the case, consider how this impacts being on the phone, or worse, email. Is it easy to see why this is so complex to explore?

I challenge you to look at communication from a different lens. Communication is incredibly dynamic. There is no fixed approach to a definition of communication. It will always depend on the context of the situation and the relative understanding between the parties engaged in it. Interpersonal communication is based on variables within the parties. Their filters drive the reception of a message, the distillation of it's meaning and then the response.

The receiver of the message has an established method of distilling the words being shared. It is this filter, if you will, that applies meaning to what is being communicated. All information coming and going is shaped by this. The filter represents the very things which make you "you." This concept will be expanded in additional chapters.

Noise or a variety of internal and external factors may interrupt the interaction. These factors are both in and out of your control. This is anything that interferes with the sending or receiving of a message. It can be physical noise (i.e. phone ringing or feeling of hunger) or psychological noise (i.e. bias or misunderstanding).

There is much which is interpreted by things not said, but rather demonstrated by body language. These are the non-verbal messages you send (i.e. folding arms across chest or not making eye contact) whether you mean it or not. These cues are very problematic due to the misdiagnoses that occur. What makes these problematic is that one body language movement or gesture can mean different things to both sender and receiver. The better way of dealing with this aspect of communication is to look for a gesture as they align with what is said, how it is said and in combination with other gestures. In other words, look for a total picture. This also implies body language is at best a flag to seek more to better understand the person and message.

The last consideration is what shapes the conversation. Context surrounds the conversation and influences the exchange. This is a very critical element. It affects how you communicate with others and is ultimately influenced by the many factors in which it occurs. It could relate to the environment and surroundings where your communication takes place. It could relate to the affinity, history or connection (or lack thereof) between sender and receiver. Also the time of day matters, as well as something unexpected. Consider how the company, team or personal elements factor in the conversation.

Tactically speaking, there are some simple ways to engage others. Management is thinking on your feet and you may only have seconds to respond to a situation. You will need to communicate action and reaction. Whether it is a discussion about performance, being late or just not getting along with others, consider some of the following tips in communication.

Shelving is one. While communicating one topic, if another person intentionally or unintentionally brings up something else off-topic, shelf it for later. Essentially your action is to acknowledge the comment, let them know we can touch on that later and then move back to the original focus.

Some of the best conversations involve questions. This is you asking questions, or questioning, throughout most of the conversation with the team member. Before you pass along feedback or judgment, ask them about their perspective and targeted action plan.

This next tactic is very practical with those team members that may be attacking your power. This involves turning the tables and asking what they might do if they were you. It relates to how they would act if they were the manager in this situation ("walking in your shoes for a moment"). "What if you were manager, I was 5 to 10 minutes late every day, how would you feel?" Remember this tactic is about putting them into another perspective. If they decide not to play along, change your tactic immediately. In fact, change direction by dealing with the behavior.

One common mistake is to give all the power to the organization by saying "well, the company really needs us to make this happen." Why would you state the obvious while at the same time reducing your own power. Simply tell them what you expect, "my expectation is...". Managers can sometimes have a tendency to use "we" in our feedback (to signify "we at..." or "we the management"). State it clearly, "I expect..." This must be communicated with a balance of focus, respect and power.

Have you ever asked someone to rate something from 1 to 10? This is a very powerful tactic. It is your opportunity to ask your team, "rate your last sales presentation" or "rate how you felt you did with the last task." It is OK to put people on the spot as long as you are trying to help your team grow. Whenever you ask for a number, always ask why they chose that number. Always follow each question with, "And how will you raise your number next time?"

There will be times when the team member gets defensive. Please do not ignore what is potentially driving this behavior. It could be anxiety, fear, lack of clarity, or even just general defensiveness. Whatever the cause, they are seeking to be heard. The most critical thing to do is to establish your listening skills. This technique represents the action of acknowledgement. "Mary, I hear your point and I know this is important to you. Let's talk about how this is affecting your performance (or focus)."

Up till now, the focus has been on the mechanics of sending. Now it is equally, if not more important to focus on the receiving aspect – Listening. Who taught you to listen? Did you take a class? Much of our abilities were more than likely influenced by trial-by-error, observation and imitation.

Reception involves hearing. This relates to the physiological application in what is happening within the receiver. This is huge, listening is difficult. It is the active distilling of incoming sounds. It is what the receiver does with what is being received. Most of us believe we are better listeners than we actually are. Despite our desire to be a "good" listener, we all embrace this skill in varying degrees of "bad". First, we were probably not formally educated in best practices. Additionally, this skill is linked to the influences discussed earlier; filter, noise, body language and context.

Now consider this, we all have currently, or have had at one time or another, listening barriers. These are things which keep us from listening effectively (e.g. judging, comparing, faking and rehearsing). So when in doubt, we fill in gaps of understanding. In other words, if you do not understand, you fill your own understanding. Quite often this can be such a personal issue. People may miss the message because they hear what they believe to be true and cannot contemplate how it could be different. To imply there is only one way to listen is to suggest there is only one way to speak. For all the varied approaches and considerations in sending messages, there must be an equal and proportionate number of ways to receive them.

How do we improve our listening? Openness involves the amount of time you allow yourself to hear something before you respond. Let go of your agenda and respect the other's point of view. Think before you say anything. Be aware that you need to listen. Take notes if you have to stimulate this behavior.

Do not interrupt. Consider active listening; especially if the other person is angry. Let the other person speak, period. Sometimes no solution is needed. Do not give advice unless asked. Make eye contact. Lean forward.

Look deeper beyond the meaning of the words, and especially into the context and intent of feelings behind the words. Pay attention to what may be at the root of the communication. Offer confirmation of understanding. Don't guess at interpretation; ask questions if you feel confused or if you need clarification.

Pay attention to non-verbal cues. This is the awareness of signs and clues of both sender and receiver. Since an estimated 55 percent of the delivery of face-to-face messages are interpreted non-verbally, be aware of how a gesture may be perceived. This can be a problematic approach due to its relative interpretation. "Tag" the gesture and ask questions.

Eliminate barriers. This represents the physical and psychological noise which may interfere with the exchange. Do not fall prey to any environmental distractions like glancing at your watch or at other people.

As you contemplate your own communication, let's end with a reality check. Not everyone with whom you communicate will have read this book or another on the importance of effective communication. They may not care. They may avoid communication. They are uncomfortable, disengaged, embarrassed or just shy. This chapter supports the development of your ability to communicate. It does not support the millions of different types of reactions or situations where you will be challenged in how and what you communicate.

If communication is less a process and more a relationship, then the next step is to embrace the imperfection in ourselves, others and the art of communication. It will be at that moment, you may let that mindset drive your ability to navigate what and how to say something. Like I stated earlier, this topic is way too broad. Start simple and grow from here.

Activities

Reflection: Define the following.

- Communication in general
- Your communication skills
- The communication within your organization

Reflection: Consider your style, skills, abilities and knowledge.

- What types of communication do you use most frequently?
- Which types are you using less?
- How much time do you spend in a day communicating verbally with others?
- How would others rate your communication?

Exercise: Think of something you love, be prepared to communicate it to someone else. Be prepared to share what, why, how and to what extent. Could it be delivered within one minute?

Discussion: Identify a recent change within your organization. List those things which were communicated effectively (clear) and ineffectively (unclear). Then list the things you would do differently with the communication of the change.

Reflection: Consider some of your most common situations. Write one of them down. Now apply something unexpected or challenging and think about how you would communicate. For example, add

- The person begins rolling their eyes, tightens their jaw, stiffens their stance

- They completely messed up and made a major mistake

- They blame someone else

- They need your grace and support

- You said something you did not mean

Take pride in how far you have come, have faith in how far you can go.

- Anonymous

2

Presence

At one time or another we have to lead someone, somewhere. We find ourselves in a place having to present a demeanor to a group of people who may or may not have knowledge of who we are and what we have to say. This is both the reality and challenge with what needs to happen next. At some point in your career as manager, you will have to stand in front of a group of people and be a leader. How would you rate?

Presence, confidence and a mindset of self-worth must emanate from a manager. It can be built and maintained. This is the goal for this chapter. It is designed to aid those who know they must manage, lead, direct, inspire and influence others. It will be especially helpful to those who are challenged with the best practices in not only projecting themselves, but also in a way that compels others into action.

Some people have a certain presence, "that certain something". How can this be defined? Maybe it is the ability to project a sense of ease, poise, or self-assurance. Maybe it is a quality or manner of a person's bearing or maybe they are of noteworthy appearance or compelling personality. Cary Grant, English actor and Hollywood icon, was said to come into a room with all eyes falling upon him. It would appear as though nothing else except him had presence within the space. And when asked about what he was wearing or what he did, no one could offer an answer. He just was. What would someone say about you if you entered a room, or more importantly, when you took center stage at a meeting or on the sales floor? One should not argue a comparison with Cary Grant. It would be comparing apples to oranges. The more important discussion is defining "presence". In an attempt to make it simple, it is what you project to others. What will be important for you is how to manufacture that projection.

When put into a situation, how do you confidently act and react? Confidence is such a key element to presence and an immensely personal thing. The reality lies with the individual and specifically how it is built or broken. I have found engaging self-confidently is doing what you believe to be right, even if others mock or criticize you for it. It is being willing to take risks, questioning concepts openly, admitting your mistakes and accepting compliments graciously.

Confidence is also found in how you use your voice. There are two things to embrace when focusing on your voice. One is voice mechanics like tone and inflection. This is the consciousness of how something is said. The other is word choice. This is the quality and quantity of spoken word. From the words you use to the way they are spoken, your ability to "make chit-chat" has direct influence to both your self-presence and the presence you reflect. You can deliver a statement and immediately create a sense of presence simply by the message you project. Please note, sometimes speaking no words can project an equally effective reflection of presence.

We also need to think before we speak. To be fair, many times we say things unconsciously. We just react and speak. We also do not consider how a word choice projects presence; i.e. I feel vs. I know, I am Worried vs. I am Concerned, I Suggest vs. I Recommend, I Might vs. I Will, We have a Problem vs. We have a Challenge. Phrases beginning with "hopefully or maybe" or inserts such as "kind of or sort of" are additional examples.

Fillers can be an irritating aspect of speech. Although, many think they are also the most fun. Irritating because this represents the "umm's" and "uhhh's" placed in between statements. The most common reason for this activity is a discomfort with silence while figuring out what to say next. This discomfort manifests itself with some type of sound used to fill the space. It is fun because if it is done with great frequency and in great numbers, people stop listening and beginning keeping count. Additional fillers are not just monosyllabic sound but also unnecessary words such as "like", "basically" and "actually".

Presence is also more than just tone, words or phrasing. Another consideration is your stance or how you stand (literally). Perhaps the better statement is how one holds one's self up or displays comfort in one's own skin. Do you recall your mother telling you to "sit up straight" or "don't slouch." Mom was and is very much right. Now that you find yourself in a workplace setting, how you stand and sit and move denotes presence and a sense of confidence. I find it very interesting to watch and observe learners in my workshops. Yes, I take note of who speaks, who does not, how they speak and how they position themselves when all of this is taking place. I see how they hold themselves as a degree of confidence. It is not always 100 percent accurate. It does promote a presence probability.

When sitting or standing, the key consideration is your upright stance, your posture. Pay very close attention to an imaginary line from your hips, up your spine, along your neck and rests at the top of your head. Do you have to "tug" on the line to get yourself upright? Slouching is very rarely perceived as positive presence. Work on your core (this is from the waist to the neck). Develop those muscles as much as possible.

Often a big question in how you present yourself is what do you do with your hands? There have been many studies about how the hands are perceived. For instance, hands in the pocket projects fear or insecurity, hands behind the back project secretiveness, and so on. I suggest being very aware of your own comfort level with your hand movement.

How well do you breathe? This impacts your stance. The diaphragm is a sheet of muscle extending across the bottom of the rib cage. It supports your lungs. It may seem very odd to suggest, but breathing and the art of breathing are some things to consciously develop and grow. Additionally, the ability to project sound is affected by the strength of the diaphragm.

For some people, the most dreaded thing is interacting with others, especially strangers. Public speaking is considered by some as one of their greatest fears. This relates to a similar fear in meeting and having to speak to total strangers. Both of these acts can be painful to observe. And yet presence is the ability to interact with one or many regardless of the circumstances.

The ubiquitous or always present large group gathering can be a tough one for "wallflowers" or shy people. You may have to speak to a stranger or someone with whom you are not familiar. First, you will need to own this mindset. Then, consciously mingle with others and initiate conversations in a friendly, interested manner. Even though you may be fearful, if you appear self-confident it becomes easier to converse with others and will also make you more approachable. Don't be afraid to join a new group or activity. You have something to contribute, and others will know it. A little stretch will help you to build confidence.

Another consideration is when you interact with your supervisor, it can be intimidating. Recent research shows that supervisors value your attitude more than your actual knowledge about your job. Project a self-assured image and engage in a positive outlook. This fosters a sense of self-worth that contributes to the image you have of yourself. You will find that others respond in a positive and reciprocal manner.

Finally, be authentic. Let me state that again. Regardless of anything mentioned in this chapter, be yourself. The information is meaningless if you have to wear these ideas like a costume. Managers can sometimes have a tendency to change who they are or what got them the promotion in the first place. The intent is now they are manager and they have to operate or act differently because they are the manager. Presence is what you project to others; especially your team. Presence comes from within.

Activities

Discussion: Consider someone with "presence". Identify their characteristics.

Exercise: Identify the following:
- Where do you find your confidence?
- Where are you most confident?
- Where do you lack confidence?

Exercise: Begin building some background for building your confidence. Identify the following:
1. Your strengths
2. Your growth areas
3. Your achievements (★ NOTE: Begin keeping an achievement and growth journal)
4. Three short term goals

Quote Discussion: Mark Twain said, "It is better to remain silent and thought a fool then to speak and remove all doubt." What does this mean?

Exercise: Identify a current issue or goal. As a group, compose key words, phrases and statements which would help one have strong presence. Then practice saying them.

Exercise: With the use of a video cam, prepare and deliver a topic. Review when completed. It is best to have a group of friends, family or peers watch, then review and give feedback.

Exercise: Read books, join a speaking organization like Toastmasters or engage in some type of educational environment to learn more about confidence building.

Even the frankest and bravest of subordinates
do not talk with their boss the same way they
talk with colleagues.

– Robert Greenleaf

3

Place

This is the part where you need to embrace there are layers to an organization. There is an organizational chart and you will fall somewhere on it. The challenge or rather the sobering moment is to realize where exactly you are, who surrounds you and how that feels. You have peers to the right and left of you, a boss above you and a team of people below you. This implies a traditional hierarchical organizational chart.

Classic management organizational platforms include Hierarchical and Cooperative. Each have a place based on the circumstances of the type of business, products and services, team dynamic, job tasks, customer realities, and a variety of other characteristics.

Hierarchical focuses on a vertical approach. It encourages not only communication, but decision making from the top down. You will find most organizational charts promote this inherently, as well as visually. This has been the predominant style taught, observed and passed down. It promotes speed, reference and constancy, while it also risks mistrust, dependence and a need for someone to influence motivation.

Cooperative focuses on a horizontal approach. It encourages communication from side to side and moreover, this communication is extensive and very open. There still exists a chain of command; however, select decisions may be made by both the individual and the collective efforts of the team. This promotes trust, unity and empowerment, while it risks speed, perspective and decision making made with or without exact or a complete knowledge.

Whatever the style or organizational chart you live by, you must know your place. At least you must know the players within the organization and how you all fit. This can be both good and bad. It may be nice to know who has the power of creating vision, making decisions, establishing policies and providing feedback.

What if that person in a position of power is not so good at their job? How are you supposed to react to their direction? What if your boss is not responding? Do you go over their heads? I say it depends on what was established in the relationship in the first place. In a way, the military has this pegged. Whether you like it or not, you know exactly at any given time who salutes and when. You absolutely know the chain of command. And without fail, you jump when the officer says jump (regardless of perception). This is not the business world.

Does your supervisor know your needs and personality traits? Do they know what makes you tick? We will cover more aspects of this later as it applies to your team. I recall my manager not knowing what I needed to hear and why I needed to hear it. Instead, he tried treating all of us the exact same way. It was my responsibility to tell my supervisor the best way to communicate and coach me since he did not figure it out on his own. That means you are ultimately responsible for your relationship with your supervisor.

For instance, let's say your supervisor has a conference call each week at the same time. They do not send an agenda and you are frustrated not knowing what will be discussed. Who is at fault? Think about this very carefully. You know your time is important and whatever may happen, you want to be part of the discussion. What are the responsibilities in this situation?

You must find your place. You are a manager of a team. You are an important part of an organization. Identify the relationships that surround you. Know who does what and how you work within each part; especially those who provide you with supervision. The hard part may be your opinion of others and how they perform their tasks. This may matter to you, but not to others. It shouldn't and if they ask, what would you say? I want that to sink in. Words matter. What matters more is how they may be interpreted.

I recall this one moment when I worked in New York for a well-known fashion house. I was part of a group reviewing a new seasonal line, the designer (yeah, the guy whose name was on the label) asked me what I thought about the line. I gave him my impression. It was a very crafted response. I was incredibly aware of every word I chose. A few moments later, my supervisor's supervisor said I gave a very good answer. I still do not know what made it so good. What exactly did I say that made it "good"?

When with peers, clients or supervisors, you must be aware of how words get interpreted and shared within a network. It is similar to the old statement "once you say it, you cannot take it back – it is out there." Everyone has an opinion about something. Think about how your opinion may be received and possibly how it might be shared. Think about the "Telephone Game" when you were a child. One person hears a word and based on their personal filter (this is something we have discussed and will discussed again further), the words take on the person's own meaning. There is an old saying which still holds true, "never say anything you would not want your grandmother to hear." Have you ever sent an email to someone, pressed send and immediately screamed "NO!" Now imagine that message was to your supervisor.

My feedback in this topic has only two areas in which to pay attention. One is simply, how you speak. This will default a bit back to the *Communication* chapter. For example, when speaking with your supervisor or even higher, think about your words very carefully. Think about the manner in which you speak; this is the tone and inflection. They are your boss, regardless of your emotional state. While this does not mean if ethics are broken to cave to their level, it does mean to be very aware of their post and how your words or actions will impact their perception of you.

The second is email or texting. This is an incredibly important means of communication at this point in our human history. I can remember when sending a fax blew my mind. Now we take for granted the transmission of thoughts, ideas and concerns in a matter of seconds and then it is sent electronically. In a matter of moments, something you sent can and will be shared with many or hundreds or thousands (well, it could also be millions). I re-read all emails despite having spell and grammar check. I re-read it and consider how the receiver might interpret the meaning of this or that phrase. Punctuation, font and spacing can have a big impact with some receivers.

I have been so blessed to have managers who ask some great questions about those things having to do with management that are not so "manage-y". They are new at their post and know only what they know. I find it very interesting that what I know and pretty much take for granted can be a new nugget of wisdom. The following are some common examples.

One of my favorites is how much does dress code matter. It matters. While to judge someone based on their wardrobe, rather than the quality and conduct of character seems wrong. It does provide insight into the degree of respect one shows for their post. I have seen new managers dress in suits and others that have pulled some wrinkled shirt and pants out of the closet. It matters that what you wear is an element of how you view the status of your post. No one expects a manager to wear the priciest or trendiest clothes possible. What is expected is attention to the fact you are the manager and your team follows your lead. You set a standard.

Another example is how a manager behaves at a company function. Bottom line is you represent your organization. Your actions will reflect both yourself and the company. Be very careful about your decisions, especially if there are things like alcohol involved. An old adage says "never do or say anything that you would regret having in a company newsletter or that your grandmother hears about". Respect for your post, skill or future is linked to how you act at the function.

A very common one is what do I do when I feel overwhelmed at times about the scope of my job? Have you ever wondered if it would be better just to go back into sales? Relax, many managers have felt or thought this. There will be times when you contemplate your post. The key responses should be breathing and communicating with your supervisor. Support must be a critical element of your organization; especially as it pertains to the responsibilities associated with your post. If it does not exist, then you may want to investigate other avenues within the organization to voice your concerns. This may be hard to read. If stress and anxiety become too large and there are no means for venting your frustration or clarifying a need for support, you may want to find another position with another organization.

The last is probably the most asked question – what do I do about managing my friends? One of the first tests and a testament to your leadership will be the transition from peer to leader. Hypothetically, one day you were their peer and the next day you were their boss. On each day which follows you have to build credibility as a boss. What you do will directly relate to how you establish your responsibility and what will be acceptable behaviorally. You must create a sense of boundary and a scope of understanding for your team. This does not mean you cannot be friendly or laugh and have fun on the job. Quite the contrary, I have found fun and accountability can work well together. You are the manager. You are the leader. You are also their friend. Each role has a place.

•

Activities

Reflection: Identify the current organizational chart for your company. Consider what you may need for further clarification.

Reflection: What if your supervisor is not responding to your needs. What happens next?

Discussion: Meet with your Supervisor and clarify the following:
- Who reports to whom?
- How is performance measured and by whom?
- What makes up the organizational chart?

And then, ask the best way to communicate with one another? Define best practices for email, face-to-face discussion, feedback, corrective action, new ideas and initiatives, problems and best time of day.

Activities

Exercise: Print one of your last emails to your supervisor or another senior leader. Share with a peer or friend and analyze how it is scripted. Is there anything you would change or improve?

Reflection: What words or mannerisms are important to your supervisor or other senior leaders?

Exercise: Pick a current issue or goal. Identify what aspects of the issue or goal are important to highlight. If you had to give an update to a supervisor, what would you say?

Life is unscripted.

                      - Very Common Saying

4

Improvisation

OK, so as manager, you must do stuff. Does what occur in any given day align with a pre-determined script or does it just happen? One of the biggest revelations a manager must embrace is that what a manager does is typically a reaction to a situation. This is a big reason for management being so improvisational in nature.

My first day as a director was surreal. I was benefiting from a high profile mentor who created a job just for me. When I began connecting with the people around me, I was invited to a lunch by my new supervisor (who was a past supervisor). While waiting for the server to take our order, he stated "I just want you to know, I resent you." Imagine the impact of that kind of statement as you begin a presumably joyous new position. How would you react?

Managers are faced with the responsibility and challenge of making decisions every day. Decision making is a process; a goal-directed, interrelated series of actions, events, mechanisms, or steps. And to be efficient and effective in decision making, it will be due to a series of behavior. I have found some of the following guiding principles in decision making to be:

- It's not always about right and wrong.

- Make decisions as you go along and do not let them gain size.

- Consider how those affected by your decision can be involved.

- Trust yourself to make a decision and then own any consequences appropriately.

- A decision made was the right thing to do at that time.

- Remember that no decision is still a decision.

There will be very specific times in your managerial life where you will have to a make a decision. You may be pressed and feeling anxious. In other words "When I am dealing with a crisis and while under stress, how can I use my creative abilities at this moment to come to a resolution?" People want their control so much. They lose sight of the tremendous opportunity of looking at things in new and exciting ways.

You improvise, you adapt and you overcome. This is an unofficial motto of the U.S. Marine Corps. It is what you must embrace as manager. Many managers seek out and pine over a type of formula that fits all situations; a type of methodology to apply when things happen. There is a method, but not one size fits all.

Managers want the "A + B = C" formula to deal with the thing. It doesn't exist and will never exist. You must change your lens, your viewpoint, your mindset. The only equation that fits or is present is "A + Variables = Customized Approach".

The "A" represents the constants in management. They are the things that must happen everyday. For example: making sales, training your team, putting out the inventory and following up with the client.

The "Variables" represent the unknown and sometimes uncontrollable things making up the day. This relates to the unplanned. For example: A team member's motivation, a client's perception of value or and anyone's relative understanding of what is happening.

The "Customized Approach" represents the action to achieve the goal ("A") based on the context of what is happening ("Variables"). This decided-upon approach is the improvisational response to getting things done through others. Managers must release the pre-conceived notions to control all things in one way or method and embrace the power of flexibility needed to be successful in today's diverse, complex and ever-changing environment.

Improvisational groups have a credo – "Just do something!" Improvisation is becoming a more and more popular learning and development target in business. Business imitates life; it is spontaneous and just happens. That is true and very powerful. That is not our challenge today. It's how to act and re-act as manager within a context.

Orienting your mindset is the first thing you must do to acknowledge the improvisational nature of managing others. It is a realization that is simple enough – life is unscripted. This chapter's intent is to orient the awareness of being improvisational. And improvisation is not only necessary, but a forgone conclusion when you decide to be a manager. Having this mindset and recognizing the relative considerations will allow you to begin to effectively and confidently engage the things which will occur.

John C. Maxwell has stated, "Change is inevitable. Growth is optional." Large or small, consider embracing change as a exciting challenge, or at a minimum, a new perspective. It is the reality of change; especially those things that occur we did not plan for or did not expect that stimulates us to access our creativity to think on our feet. So wake up not only anticipating, but seeking out places where change has or may very well occur. Proactively plan for a change somewhere in the job. When you find yourself in an unfamiliar situation, it might be wise to change the question from "what should we do?" to "what is stopping us from making a decision?" Too many reasons come to mind.

Control is relative. Generally speaking, the definition of fear is feeling out of control or having a lack of control in making decisions concerning a task, process or skill. While embracing improvisation, begin paying attention to things you do control. It has been said more than once in management circles; "control your control-ables". You always control how you respond.

Openness returns. It will impact how and what you decide. Being open is about being willing to listen to something or someone else. This means considering all possibilities before setting your course, before coming to a conclusion or rendering judgment. Willingness is the fuel for openness. Without it, one might default to freeze, flight or just freaking out. Be comfortable with the multiple possibilities in any given situation.

Context is everything. Improvisation is influenced by the context in which it occurs. Understanding and utilizing context will assist you in being more effective in planning and doing. Ask questions and seek out context before acting. It doesn't matter if it is reactive or proactive, just seek it. Ask for opinions, provide collective insight and clarify the cause-effect in all things.

Empowerment is an accelerant. All situations have relative boundaries. These boundaries can be established by the team member, policy or standard. Know them as best you can. Know your place and the extent to which you can deal with them. It is one thing to control your control-ables, it is another to your do your do-ables. Your team expects their leader to make a decision. So make it.

Learning is critical in improvisation. Mistakes happen and so do successes. You will have both. The message is learn from each. Improvisation is about both planning for the unplanned and acting upon what you have already experienced. This is a key element for the newer manager, risk decisions if for no other reason than to learn.

No matter what, own your actions. This is linked to all of the above considerations. In management, you will react to change while potentially feeling a lack control. So with a willing and learning heart own whatever happens next. Being engaged in improvisation also means being accountable for your part.

Activities

Discussion: Identify an issue you have faced, are currently facing or may very well face. List the characteristics regarding the need for flexibility, adaptation and improvisation.

Role Play: You find a key team member has informed you they will be leaving to focus on their family. They are your top producer and mentor for the remaining four team members (each with less than one year of tenure). How do you react and what do you do?

Problem Solving: A new process has been introduced within the organization. It is now in conflict with a process which has been widely used for the past six years. You have a team who is VERY familiar with the current process and begins "grumbling".

Activities

Reflection: Consider the last issue you faced. What things did you control and did not control? Were you open? What were all the facts? What was your degree of power to deal with the issue? What did you learn?

A boss creates fear, a leader confidence. A boss fixes blame, a leader corrects mistakes. A boss knows all, a leader asks questions. A boss makes work drudgery, a leader makes it interesting.

– Russell H. Ewing

5

Manager vs Leader

The day you were made manager, things changed. More than likely you were promoted due to some merit or another. Hopefully, it was not because you were the last one standing or the one least likely to steal. On Tuesday, no one cared what you had to say and then on Wednesday as manager they asked you every question possible. You answered them because you could – it's your job. At some point, you wonder...

"How do these people get up in the morning without me there?"

The definition of managing is getting things done through others. At some point a manager realizes their success or failure is tied directly to the performance of others. They know they must focus on managing processes, operations and people. They also know they must oversee clearly defined behaviors, expectations and responsibilities. Managers may do all of this lacking initiative and drive or without an ability to inspire others. Is that the leadership element?

That is the challenge. Is being a good or bad manager linked to being a good or bad leader? I say yes. And I say yes to the fact they are also two separate sets of responsibilities, two separate "hats" for two separate occasions. You do each separately and you will also be called upon to perform or wear both hats simultaneously. Now enters the question, which one is more important? They both are and at different times for different reasons.

Of all of the core competencies of being manager, managing is technically and intellectually the easiest to accomplish. It is about the job and all the tasks. The more difficult and perhaps more inspirational competency is leading; especially when you have to complete all of these managerial tasks. One of the biggest issues you may ever have to face is how to lead people. Some managers are amazing at getting the job done and completely incapable of leading a team of people. The process-side is out of balance with people-side.

It may seem that being manager is also being a leader inherently, right? It is not. They each have important specific behavioral realities. You have to be good at both. The irony or confusion is you are titled "manager". Much of this book is devoted to a perceived scope of management behaviors. The question and the challenge is how does leadership differentiate itself from management? One of my learners in St. John's, Newfoundland said "Management is what you say and leadership is how you say it." I believe that creates a clear perspective. It shows the intricacies of both the individual importance and the interdependent relationship between each.

A manager focuses on policy and process, while a leader focuses on people. A manager focuses on systems and structure, administration, maintenance and relies on control. A leader focuses on innovation, growth, development and inspires trust. A manager may imitate, while a leader will originate. A manager is guided by compliance and a leader is guided by values. A manager is caught up in the short term picture regarding how and when. A leader has a long term picture and asks what and why. Can you see the difference between the two? And can you see how both might partner given the proper context? Both need to happen.

The role of manager will always start with a complete understanding of what needs to occur every day within the job. It starts with you, your responsibilities and your capabilities to accomplish them. You must fully understand the key or core competencies required for a manager's position, as well as the team member's position. In other words, before you can manage, lead, direct, inspire and influence, you need to be proficient in all things that make a successful manager and a successful team member. This also means allowing room for errors in the job. Mistakes, problems and issues are part of the job. Emotions like stress, anxiety and anger are also part of the job. A manager must be aware of how they would engage and deal with these realities.

There is good and bad, right and wrong. Both are present and contribute in different ways. Imagine the management job is like the brain with two halves. The right side might the essential operational competencies within management. Things like Sales and Service, Staffing, Scheduling, Inventory, Systems, Auditing, Payroll, Marketing and Human Resources. While the left side represents the soft skills side of management like Decision Making, Communication, Analysis, Coaching, Delegation, Conflict, Hiring, Networking and Discipline. Many of these things may come naturally, while others may challenge you every time you face them. If you were to look at the entire landscape of tasks a manager faces, you might wonder why you decided to be one in the first place.

Many times managers do what they do best first or what is the most comfortable. They are the experts at "x", so that is their focus. They may also do what they think is the best thing to do to get the job done. Is it any wonder that senior leadership may come back and say "great, but that is not what I meant or wanted" or "yeah that's great, but what about that other thing?" It can be frustrating. Have you ever been told to do something, but not told how or why? What about your team? If you were to apply that question to your team, how would they answer? So do you have to be great at everything? No. You have to be aware of everything. Yes, you can always get better.

What are the realities of being a leader? No leader will ever tell you leadership is easy. In fact, it is wrought with many challenges. The worst or the most challenging is the feeling of superiority. Frederick the Great stated, "A crown is merely a hat that lets the rain in." Knowing that leadership can be such a challenge is the big mindset shift. This is undoubtedly the most "under the surface, most untrained" aspect of management. This is in part because the assumption is if you are a manager, you are simply "the boss, so everyone should follow you".

Leadership is the part where process is not the focus, people are the focus. While you may not appreciate your team (your people) or even like them that much, they need to be led. They expect you to be that leader, despite anything that may suggest otherwise. They expect you to know what you are talking about.

They expect you to believe in what you and they do. And they expect you to have them in your best interests. They expect a set of leadership best practices.

They expect consistency. You need to show reliable and predictable behavior. You need to create an environment whereby everyone is treated fairly and equitably. You need to dedicate to their ongoing growth and development. This may also mean scheduling time and activities with your team on a regular basis.

Consider your integrity and the team's perception of it. Simply, be authentic. You must always fulfill promises and own your mistakes. And when it comes to principles, vision, objectives and core values, be prepared to adhere to these without wavering.

Being open is allowing another perspective. It is also is similar to the saying, "Listen, Listen, Listen". This implies no matter what the situation, a leader will consider all options without bias. It also means an effort to be transparent and disclose facts with any emotions attached to them.

Teamwork is a result of leadership. Consider soliciting input, involving your team in decisions and investing in two-way feedback. Encourage peer-to-peer cooperation and problem solving. Make collaboration with the team an important part of your relationship.

Empathy starts first with an understanding that every one has value and some thing to contribute. This means exploring what is important to each individual within the team. It also means the need to show sensitivity for your team's needs and interests. It may also mean that for the first time, you begin focusing on the team before focusing on yourself.

How important is it for you to be right? Managers may fall into a trap of having all the answers all the time and no one on the team is more right than they are. This is not leadership, this making yourself divine in nature. Fallibility means you are capable of making an error. Be human and realistic with your leadership.

What is the degree of your influence? Look at inspiration as a goal by articulating a compelling vision. If motivation is the decisions people make for themselves, then it stands to reason you would engage others in discussion by appealing to their interests. A recent poll suggests one of the key reasons people leave a job is a "loss of trust and confidence in leaders". It also points out people do not leave their job or company, they leave managers. If asked how would your team rate your leadership?

It has been said a number of times by a number of people, leadership is not what you do, but who you are. Maybe that is the best way to differentiate manager from leader. The challenge though is you are often measured or evaluated by what you do. That is a critical realization in this chapter. Who you are AND what you do matters in your role. Think about this not only now in this chapter, but more so as you journey through the rest of the book. While reviewing the topics in the following chapters and their respective considerations, apply the manager – leader mindset. There will always be a time to manage and lead. You will find times they need to be separate and other times when they must be joined.

Activities

Discussion: Rank yourself on a scale of 1 to 10 (1 being low and 10 being high) as it pertains to your current management skills, abilities and knowledge. What number would you select and why that number?

Discussion: "If the only tool in your toolbox is a hammer, you will treat everything like a nail." What does this mean?

Exercise: Discuss one specific task within your job responsibilities. Then consider those things you feel you need to better manage and better lead within the task. List the behavioral elements of each.

TASK:
MANAGE   LEAD

Activities

Discussion: A recent poll suggests one of the key reasons people leave a job is a loss of trust and confidence in leaders. It also points out people do not leave their job or company, they leave managers. What does that mean?

Discussion: If a team is a reflection of a manager/ leader and if I observe your team, what would I see?

Quote Discussion: "A boss creates fear, a leader confidence. A boss fixes blame, a leader corrects mistakes. A boss knows all, a leader asks questions. A boss makes work drudgery, a leader makes it interesting." What does this mean?

Part 2:
BUSINESS

Think Different

— Apple Motto

6

Culture

Culture matters. When we were children, so many things influenced who we became. Studies show that environmental factors shape adult decision making practices by age five. Who we are and who may become is developed by the things we experience. As adults we see patterns of behavior. These patterns are the result of things such as our education, relationships and learning. Your personal culture is shaped by what has happened and what you decided to do with what has happened. Businesses are no different.

Go into any business. The minute you interact with a team member or process, an opinion begins to take shape. You immediately begin deciding to what extent this company will matter to you today and in the future. The bigger realization or perhaps more important question is, "does the company know this interaction matters?" A company is defined by its culture.

Think of your last company interaction. Bring to mind the things that happened. How would you rate the experience? How would explain the degree of experience? Do you realize your description is a direct reflection of the type of culture that business chose to allow? To be fair, a team member's decision is directly influencing your description of the experience. So culture is two things, two perspectives.

Internal perspective relates to the vibe within a company. How people are managed, communication and growth realities, as well as the quality of relationships within an organization all contribute to this vibe. This would simply be how one experiences employment within a company. The type of manager you are to others shapes the team member's perspective of your company's internal culture.

External perspective relates to the experience a customer is provided when they do business with a company. Everything from what they see when they walk in to what they hear and feel when they are engaged. The relationship created by a front line team member has impact on the business. And whatever experience I have will be the label I place on your business.

The challenge with most organizations is they may neither see nor understand one perspective or the other. They fail to see the importance both have on the business picture. Another challenge is they may see it, but do not understand the need to ensure everyone from the top down or from side to side can see what they see. They lack the collaborative environment where all team members have a shared responsibility to both support and grow the culture.

Let's make this incredibly personal. Many things affect who we are and how we conduct ourselves. Customers are no different. They seek out those businesses that add value, that are consistent, and that are convenient and friendly. They will continue to do business with an organization and tell others of their experience only if the organization lives up to the experience they expect. If your company culture aligns with and supports the customer's expectations, they will do business with you.

The study of Sociality includes a concept called Zeitgeist. It is German and literally means "time ghost". However, the phrase is used as "Spirit of the Times", or what makes up the particulars of society at any given time. In the 1940's, things were different. The world was at war from 1939 to 1945. The world was beginning to experience a global awareness and relationship. Due to the war, the gender barrier began to break down with six million women entering the workplace. Jackie Robinson broke down racial barriers in the professional athletic arena (He is one of only two athletes to have their numbers retired from all sports-Wayne Gretzky is the other). Information was becoming very important. The first computer was designed and working by 1946. It weighed in at thirty tons. There was an obvious spirit of the times. There is now as well. Society has things taking place which shape how we conduct ourselves. Businesses also have a spirit of the times.

Culture does not exist in a vacuum. It is directly the result of behavioral choices. A customer can and will sum up all that you are simply by what you do or say. It is these tangibles that cause organizations to shape and define the expectation of behavior. We will now consider some tangibles for the sake of discussion.

David Martin is a consultant. He likes Starbucks. He visited a franchise location and had a "bad" experience. He decided a call was necessary to the regional manager as a means to voice his dissatisfaction. He called and was pleasantly surprised. He will continue to do business with Starbucks. Why? The following is an excerpt from an article whereby Mr. Martin expresses what a business must consider.

"When presented with negative feedback by a customer, recognize that you may have an opportunity to actually strengthen that relationship. By first thanking customers for their business and recognizing their grievances (even without admitting "guilt") you are far more likely to keep that customer as well as gain useful feedback to improve your business.

When team members see that management actually cares about feedback, (positive and negative) they are more likely to care as well. When they see that management is personally committed to addressing issues, repairing and/or solidifying relationships, they will likely be more committed as well.

There is power in simplicity. I think Starbucks' *Green Apron Book* is a great example of this philosophy. Instead of overwhelming folks with reams of minutiae and rigid instructions, it gives guiding principles (and a few simple examples) of the environments they hope to create and legendary service they strive to provide."

So what makes a culture a culture? It has to be more than a clever phrase or lofty aspiration. It needs some type of substance or tactile quality. It requires very specific, definable behavior. It needs tangibles.

I recently got my oil changed. I was distracted and in a hurry. I went to a location where I typically have my oil changed. They warmly welcomed me. They opened the door and offered me a cup of coffee. I noticed the new décor in the waiting room. I had to use the washroom. It had a new type of floor and fixtures. It was extremely clean. They had a new flat screen on the wall and I was able to connect to free WiFi. Stop for a moment and deconstruct the scene. What tangibles were being used or in place to create a customer experience. Did they matter? I asked the main guy about the new changes in the waiting area and washroom. He said they had changed them because they had found out what mattered to customers – it was the waiting environment in addition to getting the oil change done quickly. Do you understand these subtleties? I will go back to that location every time and tell everyone about how cool it is there.

These subtleties are simply very specific things which are designed to occur with every customer (and team member) each and every day. They are defined, trained, coached, measured and reinforced. They are the day-to-day behavioral tangibles within an organization. Culture without tangibles is just a philosophical vision. Culture with tangibles allows customers the ability to experience the vision and to either like or dislike the organization. So in a way, every organization designed to interact with a customer must define what they expect to happen to support the desired vision and objectives. These things, these tangibles must have structure. More on this in the next chapter.

Activities

Discussion & Exercise: Take time to question how your team member's perceive the customer experience.

Reflection: Take time to consider how your team members rate the culture of the company.

Exercise: Brainstorm with your team on how the industry has changed recently. Ask what is important to customers given the current scene.

Then define what things within the organization support these types of concepts in customer experience and service. Be sure to align how your tangibles align with the group's points.

Exercise: Using provided paper and pens; instruct your team to draw their perception of the organization's culture by using images, symbols and artistic representation only. It is creative in nature. No feedback will be given. You have to be OK with the results.

Exercise: Make a list of the tangibles within the organization (i.e. dress code, training, job descriptions, selling steps, etc.). Then have your team rate to what extent those are clearly defined and instilled into the company culture.

I will deal with them according to their
conduct, and by their own standards I will
judge them.

- Ezekiel 7:27 (NIV)

7

Core Values

In 2004, Best Buy decided something interesting. They decided to change their model from being price-centric to being people-centric. They clearly identified five specific customer profiles and began training their teams into how to best communicate with them and work toward their solutions. They invested millions into a select number of pilot stores to implement this new model. After a year, they had outperformed those stores not in the pilot by about five percent in total year-end same stores sales gain. While the percentage may seem low, it is huge when measuring in millions. The specifics of this case study may be found on the Best Buy website in their investors section. Why tell this story?

Retail is detail. I learned this in the late eighties when I took my first retail management job. Best Buy decided not to compete on the big scale like price. Everyone was doing that and watching their margin dip. Best Buy took a stand and identified that it is the details the customer brings into the store which matters most. If a retailer can clearly identify a need and then accurately provide a solution for that need, the customer will respond and even in some cases spend more than they intended to in the first place. This is not earth shattering. It is actually common sense.

When I walk into a business, something happens. If I own the business, I want something to happen. If I own many locations within the business, I want a series of consistent things to happen in all locations. As the business grows, so does my intensity of headaches regarding consistency. Think of your favorite store or company. How many locations are there? Are they consistent? The question is not if they are good, are they consistent?

Every business has some type of defined expectation when a customer engages them. This does not mean they are successful in accomplishing these expectations. What are expectations? Expectations are tangible behaviors. They are standards within the business. A standard is defined by Merriam-Webster as something set up and established by authority as a rule for the measure of quantity, weight, extent, value, or quality. If you get paid a salary, a company expects you to do something in return at a certain time for a certain entity. This is a behavioral rental agreement.

In the *Culture* chapter, the goal was to illuminate the importance of culture and its relative meaning in the business-world. This chapter is about standards. Standards shape the type of culture we aim to achieve. In a way, business is defined by its expectations.

As manager, you may not make strategic decisions, but you do require the definition of what you are striving to achieve and more importantly, the means to achieve it. Imagine your post. Think about all the things you do in a day. Your decisions need to be aligned with a goal and objective to meet a particular need. This is where standards are born. What vision, objectives and structure is required to get you, your team and your customer to that place?

Another consideration is when a team member starts, what happens? This comes back to the discussion of understanding both internal and external culture and their relative importance to a bigger cultural picture. Culture is difficult to support without standards. This would be regarding the organization's standards of conduct with both customers and team members.

The standards we provide our team members influence the length of time they are willing to spend with us. Team members dictate what a business needs and will only remain with those who consistently execute against those needs. The standards we provide our customers will influence the business that we do with them. Customers dictate what a business needs and they will only do business with those who consistently execute against those needs. They want accurate information and advice, clear communication, complete service (one-stop), variety of options, and a relationship (experience) which does not change from one time to another.

Therefore, standards start with clarity and definition. In an effort to keep it simple and to increase operational efficiency, sales productivity and customer loyalty, the following are categories for implementation: Efficiency and Experience standards.

Efficiency Standards make up the way in which we conduct our business. Some may even say these are the standards below the surface or what is typically taken for granted. Think about your day-to-day responsibilities, what things could you do better? Think about your team member, what can be done to make their hands-on part of the business more efficient?

These by the way are the easiest to create, implement and enforce, or rather they should be. If you cannot get someone to do these, it may be much harder to get them to do more complex and skills-based standards. These standards will typically involve some type of process or procedure. It will be important to detail what makes up proper and flawless execution.

Experience Standards are efforts to impact the customer experience and increase sales. This is where specific and targeted sales behavior takes precedence. How many of you have had a sales person completely fail at sales? How many of you were told to increase your own sales productivity and not quite sure where to start or which behavior to complete? These standards are about clarifying sales behavior every time on the sales floor and with every customer.

Essentially these standards are designed to reinforce the customer experience and keep a customer for life. These standards require skill and training. They will also require repetition, reinforcement, coaching, feedback and ideas. If you want a sales increase, just putting these standards on the wall will not help. Your people will need ongoing support and development.

Here is another consideration; is there a difference between sales and service? And if so, which comes first? Which is more important? There is no simple answer. However, in an effort to eliminate as much noise as possible, let's look at each of these questions and their respect answers as simply as possible.

First, there is no difference between sales and service. They are each customer-facing scenarios with revenue generating opportunities. They involve clear communication with empathy, an awareness of customer needs, a positioning of some type of solution and training to develop a behavioral skill set.

Second, in a literal world, a sale comes first and service is anything that follows the original sale. One may argue, that if times passes and a customer comes in for service, it is not sales. To set the record straight, a sale did in fact come first regardless of time. The bigger or more important statement is the customer deserves a high degree of interaction at all times to create a complete experience.

Lastly, they both are important. Each has an impact on the bottom line, which in turn is fed by customer satisfaction and retention. Think of it this way, your leadership impacts how a sales consultant sells and serves – each incredibly important to the business. Your efforts secure customers for life.

So what does a standard need to be effective? Have you ever been told to do something but not told how or why? Here is where you need to be a manager of clarity. Anytime you request a thing or action of your team, be it a standard or process, it is incredibly important to share more than just the task itself. You must be prepared to share what it is you expect, why it is important to complete, how you expect it to be completed, how you intend to support the adoption of it and to what extent it needs to be done or measured.

For example, let's say you have two new standards. One is "Every team member must come to work on time and be fully prepared for their shift." The other is "Every team member must greet or acknowledge every customer." While these may not fit the nature of your business, look at the support which is needed to support any standard. You have identified the what. You have not clarified the how. Each must involve behavioral specifics. This is ultimately what good looks like. Next, you must supply the why or the reason behind the standard and its relative importance to the individual, team, customer and overall organization. Then, it must be very clear what you the manager will do to support the execution of the expectation. This would include but not be limited to communication, training, coaching, reinforcement, follow-up, recognition and reward. Lastly, the standard must have some type of degree of completion. This can be some type of score or metric. Is the standard winning or losing?

At some point standards must evolve. Yes, a new set may emerge due to a changing market or customer need. There must also be an evolution from telling a team to accomplish the standards to doing them because they are second-nature and just the right thing to do. This is the movement from standard to core value.

Consider the word "standard". Now consider the word "core value". What is the difference? The implication is the movement from directing to owning a task. Referencing Disney, it is the difference between policy and tradition. They have policies, but refer to them as traditions. Do you see a difference? They also train their cast members in every way to execute their tasks while meeting their vision of "creating a fun, fantasy-like experience for the family" and exemplifying courtesy, efficiency, show and safety. How does a company get to this distinction? Disney invests in their people (cast members). They train and develop them constantly and they hold them accountable to their role and tasks. "One and done" cannot be your team development credo if your goal is to move your self, your team and your organization into core values.

What are your organizations core values? If you do not have them, then you probably do not have defined standards. Core Values cannot occur without defined expectations and standards. The most important question of this chapter is not about core values or if you have standards. It is if your team on the front line were asked if they had a set of defined standards, what would they say? And if they said something, what would it sound like? The answer is the extent of your culture.

Activities

Reflection: Think of a business you frequent. Do they have standards? Are they obvious or subtle? Are they an accident or a result of careful consideration?

Action: With the next standard or initiative to be implemented, make the following notes prior to the communication with your team:

- What is exactly being asked?
- How is it to be implemented?
- Why is it being implemented?
- What will you do to support implementation?
- To what extent will the implementation be measured?

Exercise: Ask your team what standards exist within the organization. Do not lead them in any way. Let them share what they think. Collect the answers. Review them and share your thoughts.

Activities

All we have to decide is what to do with the time that is given us.

– Gandolph The Grey

8

Prioritization

When waiting for a flight at an airport, I asked "How long till we board?" The gate agent answered "Any minute". Twenty minutes later, I asked again and the answer was the same. In my fury, I realized the brilliance of the answer. They were perfectly right, it could any minute; any minute within the next hour or the next or tomorrow for that matter. Time fills an exact construct. It is exactly the same amount of seconds and hours and days in any given week or month. When we look at the stuff that needs to be done, we look at those minutes, hours and days to fit everything in.

You get a call from your Regional Manager who states you have to change your schedule to be part of a store manager training program. It starts in two days and this is the week you just came back from holiday. You are putting a new hire through their training program and your best sales consultant won that trip to Mexico and won't be back until after you leave. You are concerned about this because your store is not hitting its numbers and it is the third week of the month. How do you map out your two days?

This chapter will challenge your understanding of your tasks and prioritization skills. There will be no planner or specific time management tool, although for some of you, having these kinds of tools will help you make better decisions. We will instead look at how you utilize your abilities efficiently and put your tasks in proper perspective.

You see everyone wants time management. The issue is not the time part, although some may argue they do not have enough time. No one can change that. You have the exact amount of time Einstein, Shakespeare and Steve Jobs had and have. So it must be the management part that people want. If that is the case, a tool may help. That is not what you find here. I have found the key part of time management is how a manager prioritizes their tasks. That is what you must explore. When prioritizing, you must make decisions.

What challenges managers? In a word, balance. It is true that time management is one of the hardest jobs in management. With this position comes the inevitable aspect of juggling many tasks at once. This may be said about any job on the planet. All that must be done in a day or week always seems to be a priority.

In an effort to find some sense of balance, we will investigate and clarify those things which must have precedence in our given day. It is one thing to wallow in the misery of not having enough time, but true time management is only possible with a complete awareness and understanding of tasks and their prioritization.

Regardless of what you do in life, you will prioritize something. The key will always be to look at your day and week and begin scheduling those things that are essential to your success. You then must make those days precious by informing everyone that certain tasks will be scheduled at specific times during the day and week. Always consider the following questions:

- What is essential? This is more consciously looking at your tasks. Check for any redundancies or systems inefficiencies and eliminate if possible.

- What can be delegated? Managers become "task hoarders" out of fear and struggle with time as a result. The fear is no one can do it better, faster or with as much accuracy as you.

Also if they do it wrong, you still have to do it. Pay very close attention to this statement!

- What is your greatest asset? Identify your assets as a starting point when prioritizing. The absolute asset in your company is your people. Without which your business suffers. How do they factor in your day?

- What brings you the biggest return? Clarify your desired results. Explore all benefits to you, your team and your business.

After you have established the above criteria, begin mapping your days and weeks. Be sure to take mission critical tasks and make them "sacred" – dates and times whereby the tasks become concrete, consistent and habitual. Imagine consistent individual coaching on every Tuesday between 2:00 and 4:00 p.m. What impact do you believe that would have to the overall organization, to the scope of core values, as well as cementing a cultural foundation?

I believe all managers want to create sacred time for themselves and their team. But other stuff gets in the way. So what process dictates how you make decisions? We will keep this part simple. Decisions come in all shapes and sizes. They can hinge on the emotional, psychological, relational or ethical. No, let's just make it about business tasks. We will define a plan for dealing with time management by looking at the mindset and methodology in decision making.

Most people have heard about the 80/20 Rule. It is also known as the Pareto Principle. It is named after an Italian economist, Vilfredo Pareto. He created a formula after observing that twenty percent of the people owned eighty percent of the land. Later in the 1940s, Dr. Joseph M. Juran expanded the 80/20 Rule. He observed that 20 percent of something always is responsible for 80 percent of the something else.

For example, you can apply the 80/20 Rule to almost anything. In sales, 80 percent of your sales will come from 20 percent of your sales staff. In addition, 20 percent of your staff will cause 80 percent of your problems. It works both ways.

The value of the Pareto Principle for a manager is that it reminds you to focus on the 20 percent that matters. In theory, of the things you do during your day, only 20 percent really matter. Those 20 percent produce 80 percent of your results. Whether the numbers actually play out that way or not, identify and focus on the critical things. When the fire drills of the day begin to sap your time, remind yourself of the 20 percent you need to focus on. Bottom Line, don't just work smart, work smart on the right things. How would you identify your 20 percent?

At one time or another, you will face a decision which will take planning. You will need to construct a plan for making it happen. Decision making needs a map of some kind. This represents a prescribed chain of events or considerations to affect a choice and decision. Making decisions based on both targeted priorities and the things which affect them is where leaders excel. Consider the MAP IT concept.

Mission represents the "why" behind the "IT". Many times a goal or objective is only given. It may lack the basis, background, issue or scratch needing to be itched. Define the cause and what is at the root of the goal and objective.

The next element is Assess. This is the "context" surrounding the "IT". It is the time spent looking at what is present in the current scene as you begin planning. Assess the perceptions, the assets and any potential roadblocks before you plan any implementation.

Plan is the implementation. It is the "what, how, when and who" in getting it done. It is also the "follow up" required for "IT". Determine all elements to take action; especially defined behaviors with targets, support and measurement.

Regardless of all the prioritization and planning, questions will arise. What do I do with all the stuff that always seems to come up? Stuff will always come up. I have found the easiest way to deal with the unexpected is to allow it into your day before it happens. Be proactive by planning to be reactive. If you have a day representing 100 percent of your time, identify the percentages. Plan the 40 percent of tasks you always have no matter what and then add a hypothetical 40 percent of things which will probably come up. Then the remaining 20 percent is your "wiggle" room to plan the additional stuff which needs to be planned. These numbers are fictitious but you get the idea.

Another reality is priorities change. What impact does that have on myself and the team? You get to answer that one. The team wants you to be the leader. They will look at you, observe how you respond and mirror that. Change is inevitable. We are designed to change. While we do not control the changes which occur, we do control the way we react during change.

Delegation is probably on of the toughest things for a manager to embrace. It is ultimately about giving up a little or a lot of control. What if I delegate something and they do it wrong? Well, help them to do it better and do not take it back. Train and trust.

Activities

Reflection & Exercise: Make a list of what you do in a given day and week. First make the list and then identify those things that are essential – these must be done to operate the business. After that, identify the ones may be delegated. After that, identify the ones which are critical for the business. The idea is to establish how you prioritize both your time and tasks.

Exercise: Plan "sacred" actions and activities in your schedule. Communicate them to your supervisor and ensure they conform to the concept and will fit into the scope of your schedule.

Discussion & Exercise: Either with a group of peers or your supervisor, identify a important topic and apply a selection of "what if" possibilities. Brainstorm ideas for managing or leading within them.

Action: With the next or any new initiative, use this MAP IT method to plan implementation. Share your thoughts and notes with your supervisor.

Activities

You have to have confidence in your ability,
and then be tough enough to follow through.
                                    – Rosalynn Carter

9

Accountability

This is, can, will, should and must be the one of the biggest tasks of manager. As a new manager, a first step is to clarify the overall job expectations. This involves you getting to know the scope of the job. Is it clearly defined? How are the manager's efforts to be measured clarified? What a manager may miss at the beginning is to ask some fairly important questions about accountability. If ever there was a great question to ask a prospective employer or a supervisor about a management job, it is "How will I be held accountable?"

Now put this in the context of managing others. The same two extremely important steps need to be clarified to your team. Nothing is more frustrating to a team member than to either not be told what is expected or not told how the expectations will be measured. Even worse would be that neither one is clarified.

Now let's take it up a notch. Imagine one of your best team members is late for a shift. They know the policy. They understand it and have even signed off on it. They really have no excuse at all. They are about 23 minutes late and it is a first time. How would you respond? Managers with good intentions (and bad ones for that matter) make choices concerning this topic. Usually, it comes in the form of a questions like "How important is this really?", or "Will this impact their overall performance?" You may very well be right, it really isn't a big deal. It probably will not impact their performance overall. It will always be your call. Who sees your decision? Remember that.

What happens if it is a poor performer and it is their third time being late without excuse? Does the decision change? Yes, it should for a number of reasons. One, it is a third offense. Two, if they are a poor performer, this implies they are not meeting some type of criteria which makes them "poor". This will always influence action. Lastly, they did not attempt some type of contact as to the being late. Are the two different? Who sees that?

Here is the issue – the balance between account-ability and following through. Can you see how one response may impact the other? By one action, you have directly influenced the other. In this case, favor-itism may be seen by others, thus eroding both your power and integrity. I will not dispute that inconsis-tencies and favoritism do exist. These are the realities in accountability.

The essence of accountability is related to perfor-mance and efficiency and is critical to the success of any organization. You cannot decide one day to "let's just sell" or "let's just be efficient" without considering the reality of an organization's needs. There must be considerations and decisions in aligning and re-align-ing priorities. This will relate specifically to individu-als and in teams of individuals as to what is expected and how the whole is being held accountable.

Which is better: two people out of eight who ensure the team is over target or all eight adding to the team being over target? This can be a hard part of managing your performance to a goal. Do you focus on the few who you know can hit the numbers or do you work with the team to hit the goals? The easy answer is that everyone is accountable and should be held to a fair and equitable standard. The hard part is dealing with a path of least resistance when under stress.

The reality is everyone is accountable. Your super-visor is accountable for their teams. You are responsible for your team's performance. Your team has the responsibility to provide the activity for that performance. Each plays a huge part in the overall success of the organization.

Accountability is about ownership. Leadership decided to make you manager. Someone felt you had merit. They felt your skills, abilities and knowledge were sufficient enough to be manager and to ensure productivity. So own the responsibility. The way you manage pays for your own position's reason for being.

Mediocrity is not a measurement of accountability. Where do you stand on this; to just get by or to always strive to excel? The only goal is to exceed performance and productivity goals, as well as customer expectations. This is harder than it seems. It takes tenacity, discipline and awareness.

When considering these truths, you must begin to ask questions regarding how each has an influence in your management job. It is not a question of which one matters most. They all do. It's an awareness of these principles as you manage your team. Moreover, as a new manager, it may not be evident what makes up the key areas for accountability or degrees of accountability. Most organizations will have some sort of measurable means for accountability. It will be either very obvious or some industry-specific metric. The ultimate consideration for accountability will be based on the thing that matters most to the business.

There is general productivity. This can be seen as sales and service or the nature of getting your team's job done. This will include any targets you and your team are meant to achieve. You would be accountable for the number within your group who is below, at and above target. This may be associated with raw data (quantity-totals) or a calculation of the data (quality-percentages to total).

Operational performance will also be a layer of accountability. This would relate to time, reduction rates, compliance percentages and degrees of effectiveness. Are you and your team getting the job done within a reasonable cost to the organization? This could be payroll cost or inventory effectiveness.

There is also the people-side of accountability. This is everything from training to coaching. How many in your team are certified or fully trained? Do they have what is needed to be successful? It is about succession planning and performance reviews. Every team member must have benchmarks within their team member life cycle (more on this in another chapter).

Accountability can be seen as a tough word. Holding someone accountable infers a certain amount of subjugation. Sometimes people just do not relate very well to that kind of relationship. The challenge for you will be to what extent you are able and willing to hold another person accountable. It is also important to note, you must hold yourself accountable. This does not work if everyone else is accountable, and not you. You are the boss and you must hit your goals and targets. I was once told "If you are fired for not hitting your targets, will your team still continue to pay your salary? So how much do you love your team?" Do not read this so literally. It is OK to love or have value for the people with whom you manage. The suggestion within the shared comment is your success or failure is tied the performance of others. The others are your team. It pays to hold them to the quantity and quality of their job at an absolute minimum.

What about accountability when it involves failure, deficiency or non-compliance? This could be a tough one for a manager. The exact outcome and context will be critical in what happens next. Is the outcome a hiccup or habitual? Is it something tied to a personal issue or an issue of willingness? It is very difficult to state the best action as the situation may be constructed of multiple possibilities. I will offer these three considerations. First, trust your gut. I have shared that on hundreds of occasions common sense prevails. The situation and everything surrounding it will feel a certain way and you will immediately know the answer. Second, when in doubt, ask someone. Share the situation with your supervisor, peer or even a loved one to gain some insight. Lastly, you may have to move to coaching or even a stronger path like discipline. These topics are both within the book.

Activities

Discussion: Define the concept of accountability within your organization. Think about the comments made by senior management as well as the front-line team members.

Discussion: Consider accountability and how it factors in certain situations. Use the following categories to start. You will need to select specific situations within each.

- Performance (e.g. Sales, Service, etc.)

- Operations (e.g. work station, computer usage, etc.)

Group Exercise: Discuss and note one specific area of accountability within your job scope. Then discuss and note the measures that fall within the accountability.

Area of Accountability:

Measurement:

Activities

Group Exercise: Identify those things needed in order to support accountability. What makes someone more accountable than not?

If you cannot measure it, you cannot manage it.
- Management Adage

10

Analysis

If managing is ultimately a commitment to growing and developing others, there must be some degree of measurement to qualify your success and dependence on your team. Let me say that again. Your winning or losing the game is directly linked to what a team member does or does not do statistically.

No matter what business you are in, you are being measured. The degree of measurement changes based on what is being measured and who is measuring it. For example, a CFO measures the overall performance and profitability of their organization. A Vice President will look at their respective business channel. While as manager, you are required to measure the daily metrics of what occurs at your specific location. This means not only looking at the overall numbers, but also to review individual performance.

So what do you measure? With most organizations, you first and foremost measure sales or some type of conversion of services or actions. Your daily or weekly goal is to influence productivity, efficiencies and compliance. You are being measured on your ability to accomplish those goals.

The challenge is about the best and most accurate method of measurement for both process and people. What are the foundational statistical resources at your disposal? Our task will be to ensure you fully understand not only their relativity and meaning, but also the importance of how analysis of the metrics plays a part of your overall success. Your task is identifying the best method for tracking those metrics.

The value of measurement and the analysis includes how you can objectively see your performance by location, individual, time frame and category. It involves your team seeing not only how they are performing as individuals, but also as a collective. It provides insight as to how close or far away you and your team are from a desired destination. If the targets and the measurement criteria are clear, you can increase your team's level of commitment (or Buy-In). In some cases, to measure is to motivate. The old saying is, "inspect what you expect."

In business, there are very common statistics to measure. The goal is always to provide some type of observation on execution of sales and service behavior, identification of growth areas of opportunity and a provision of scores or metrics for measurement. All organizations have ways to collect, distill and distribute productivity data. It can be KPIs (key performance indicators) like closing ratio, average sale, turn-around-time, productivity per hour or gross margin. You have the responsibility of tracking your performance metrics. Although measurement is important, not all statistics can be easily tracked or easily analyzed for meaning (this discussion will come later). In fact, it is the statistics that cannot be as easily tracked that causes managers to think "If it can't be tracked on the POS (point of sale or main system of tracking performance) system, it probably isn't very important to me."

Operational compliance is difficult to track systematically and more easily tracked through observation. It sounds confusing. If you are implementing an efficiency standard like dress code, you cannot track it through some type of system. However, either some-one is doing it or not! The big challenge is how you can be objective with tracking the overall results. The goal is always to align your data as a trend. Whether it is by a percentage or number of times, you will need to see the progression of compliance. That becomes your statistic and represents a base measurement showing to what extent you accomplished your efforts. A compli-ance scorecard represents a system of measurement and is the strength of this organization in recording degrees of efficiency within your operations.

If you are measuring the success of your culture and standards, the customer can provide feedback. Customer surveys have a specific perspective. The re-ality is every customer's perspective is influenced by their experience. They make real-time and all future decisions, by that experience. One question with a customer survey is how objective is the data if they are happy. Of course they will say nice things. What if they did not have a good experience? Does this give you an objective look into the exchange? It can. The key is to use all the surveys and analyze them for key trends and opportunities. When do you get their feed-back? Timing of surveys will be important to consider. Also, will a customer need some type of enticement to provide their thoughts?

Mystery shopping feedback and measurement of the customer experience provides an additional perspective. Another question is again how objective is this format? Does the "fake" customer know what is expected or what to really look for? Again, the key is to evaluate for trends. It represents data to support if the team is doing it or not at a given time. This is why mystery shopping is yet another way to extract a measurement of customer service. Mystery shopping and customer surveys are very similar in their goals.

Implementing this type of program usually entails bringing in some type of third party (although having your aunt help also qualifies). There are a number of organizations that focus on this in general and within your own industry. Ideally, your goal is to have an non-emotional third party come in and report on their experience based on pre-selected and targeted criteria. At the end of the day, like customer surveys, the data you compile will be based on impressions, relative understanding and memory. It may also be, in some cases, emotionally charged.

Tracking performance becomes the most objective way to measure the overall performance of the team and the team members. It is exactly here that you are able to confidently discuss the skills and ability of your team members with facts in hand. You may even find out, by tracking, your team will begin to reach for your support because of the statistical data.

One of the critical aspects of holding your team accountable is by visibly posting their performance. This should be as consistent a presence in the work space as having desks, chairs and the coffee pot. When we speak about the importance of posting results, we are making accountability to performance a critical element of employment. If you have multiple locations, your effort to gain consistency in reporting and presentation of results will need to be standardized.

Will analysis be seen as micro-management? It can be if your only goal is to look at each individual every moment of everyday. The more you put them under a microscope, the more you affect their levels of commitment and buy-in. Your focus in posting this information is to show the team how the store is doing against a goal or goals. More specifically, this information acts as a roadmap to a desired location.

More than that, your team will want to know their individual score as it relates to the collective. They are often times competitive, worried, excited, scared or just curious to know their score. Of course the score is either a question of "quantity or quality". Will analysis cause competition? It can, and by the way, that is precisely what you want on a selling floor. If the game your team is asked to play is fair and equitable for all participating sales consultants, and if you are clear and consistent about your reasons why you are tracking performance, your team will enjoy the challenge.

Remember, statistics are not opinions. There are two other absolutes as it pertains to statistics. One, they are historical. In effect, they happened – past tense. Two, they do not just happen. They are at the effect of something else; namely behavior. One might surmise both of these points imply a difficult or at least challenging path in analyzing statistics for meaning.

Statistics are the result of behavior. If a team member has a low number in something, it is due to something they are doing or not doing to cause the deficient statistic. The biggest challenge in driving performance is isolating the real reason behind a team member's behavioral choice. At the surface, the solution may seem exceeding easily to diagnose; however, something quite different may be working under the surface. Any manager can come up with the formulaic approach and action plan to fix the issue. The manager may very well become frustrated if the symptoms and behavior still exist after their coaching.

The goal of the manager is to focus on the causal factors behind statistics. Anyone can simply read some numbers and quickly ascertain either a positive or negative outcome. The manager who can understand the numbers and the behavior fueling the individual's choice will be much more successful in improving their efficiency and performance.

Therefore analysis needs another element for it to have impact on the performance of a team or team member. Everything in life and especially numbers exists within a context. First comes an understanding of how things will be measured. The second will be the understanding of the number or outcome and how it plays a part in the business. The last will be the cause for the number or outcome. To help with these perceived challenges, managers can simply follow a logical chain of events or an understood reasoning behind statistical outcome. If some type of ratio or measurement is down, simply look at all skills, abilities and knowledge associated with each step of a selected cycle. This will be explored deeper in the next chapter.

Activities

Exercise: To ensure complete understanding, identify one of your standards and discuss the following for each: What is the key performance metric being measured and What methodology is being used to collect the data?

STANDARD:

Key Performance Indicators?

How would you collect?

Discussion: Meet with your regional manager and explore your understanding of each of these metrics. Be prepared to do some homework if you are unclear about the measure and how it is calculated.

Discussion & Exercise: During a meeting with your team, ask your team the ways in which they feel they are being measured. Capture the data and review it with your supervisor.

Action: Plan a portion of time during a week where you will interview select customers and evaluate their overall experience. This is call the Maitre d' survey – check their experience as would a maitre d' at a restaurant.

Role-Play: Consider the following:

During the course of a day, one of the sales consultants asks you to help them on the difference between coverage and rate plans of the competition. They state that they have been missing sales as they struggle with what "they" offer and feel that it is very hard to make new activations as a result of the competition. They have also heard about the varying compensation and incentive programs of the competition. They feel that the competition has the advantage. It is the end of the month, the store has been struggling and this sales consultant is not going to hit their numbers. What do you coach?

Part 3:
OTHERS

The answer to the question managers so often ask of behavioral scientists – 'How do you motivate people?' – is, you don't.
                                        - Douglas McGregor

11

Causality

Being a manager involves some type of commitment to growing and developing others. It is more than a task, it has to be a mindset for you to excel. You must attach it to your drive to be successful. As manager, your success is dependent on the success of your team. Here is the thing, if success and growth are targets, then a greater understanding of what drives (or does not drive) people must precede it. Is it the person and their motivation or their abilities to do their job?

A challenge in managing others is the understanding associated with both performance and people. The main target in this section will be to look at your process of assessing productivity and efficiency as it is directly linked to a person's abilities and choices. The idea will be how a better understanding of behavior can directly impact each team member's overall performance as well as creating an environment where people want to work.

While this seems like a simple task, it is not. Choice is up to the one choosing; which means you have to uncover what is behind the choice to either recognize it or re-construct it. As managers, you have been tasked with driving sales performance and operational efficiencies through the efforts of your people. The importance of a coaching mindset is critical. It must be stressed that you have requirements, standards which need to be fulfilled every day when leading your team. This ultimately is your commitment to the coaching and development of your team.

Another way to look at this is a reality of goals which shape your immediate understanding of "why" to coach. While this may seem like a simple coaching task, it is not. Consider the team member who hits their goals. Now think about the team member who is a low performer, or perhaps worst, a team member who is inconsistent all over the place? Coaching has a basis in the growth and development of the team member, especially as it aligns with the goals of the business and the cost of performance (especially poor performance). Simply put, it is your job and your livelihood. Your success, your bonus is directly tied to the efforts, choices and productivity of others.

Making coaching a priority allows everyone a chance to be successful. If a team member is getting ongoing feedback on their performance, they make better decisions. They can change this, continue with that or train to improve something else. It is this direction and influence which ensures capability, ability, habit and motivation. By knowing their job (and the quality of the job) and by knowing their score (and the quantity of their job), they may actually stay longer.

What is coaching, really? This is a tough one. Managers want to know what style, method or type of coaching will yield the best or quickest results. Yeah, well, all of them will and for different reasons based on the context of the situation. Imagine you have a team member who is trending down in performance. They have been strong and all of a sudden, they are not performing. You have observed them in the past and know them to be fully capable. You ask them about it, they say "I'm sorry, I will work on it." With a little time, they are still struggling and you sit down with them. They reluctantly say they are having problems at home. What do you coach?

As manager, causality takes shape when you look at a measured outcome and evaluate it as high or low. Regardless of the number, there will always be a contributing or causal factor. If my accessory attach rate is below target, I did something to cause that. Also bear in mind another reality, two people can have similar results and for entirely different reasons.

During the course of a day, one of the sales consultants asks you to help them on the difference between coverage and rate plans of the competition. They state that they have been missing sales as they struggle with what "they" offer and feel that it is very hard to make new activations as a result of the competition. They have also heard about the varying compensation and incentive programs of the competition. They feel that the competition has the advantage. It is the end of the month, the store has been struggling and this sales consultant is not going to hit their numbers.

The possibilities based on the context of the situation could be knowledge (or a lack of it), fear of not hitting their numbers, an issue with overcoming objections or not being aware of the competition's product or plan offerings. There could be many more involving both professional and personal roots. This is the challenge. Managers must ask or at least uncover "Why?"

The simple answer is skill versus will. People don't wake up wanting to fail. So why is it they don't get it done? Each answer to this question comes with a different focus and nuance. There are a number of ways to influence and direct behavior. If you have been focusing on the growth and development of your team, it implies you have been training and coaching towards their success. At some point, there may be a question about their skill or will.

All behavioral choice has an influence; something that stimulated the action. As manager this comes to your attention after analyzing business outcome. This realization is also defined as a cause-effect relationship (a.k.a. Causality). As simple as it sounds, it may be a complicated influence or root cause. This is where your ability to choose the correct action plan will be tested. There are four common influences and root causes.

Training is about capability or "I don't know how". The team member may not have the knowledge required to understand and/or properly execute the behavioral expectations associated with the statistical goal. If the outcome is deficient, this individual may be lacking the development or training needed to be successful. This is the most common behavioral cause. Investigate knowledge, skill and understanding.

Architecture refers to the team member's ability to achieve the goal that may be hindered by some obstacle. Think "I can't". If you have selling expectations with a reliance on something else, it may impact and affect performance. This may be associated with process, procedure or systems. Investigate aspects of the business like scheduling, systems inefficiencies, any disconnect between departments (i.e. home office and your location) or ineffective communication.

Adoption has a very common reason behind it, habit or time involved in change. Typically, it may manifest itself in your team as either "I am not there yet", "I am used to doing it this way" or "that is the way they've always done it." This is allowed when managers do not follow up, give feedback, role-play or hold their team accountable. Further investigation may illuminate the time involved since exposure to the task, existing habits, lack of feedback and coaching or the degree of your consequences-based environment.

Mindset is intrinsically linked to one's willingness or "I won't". A team member may be apathetic or have limited to no value for the goal when you hear "I just forgot" or "It's not important". Something else may be more important than achieving the statistical goal. This person may simply be de-motivated or have a conflicting motivation. People motivate themselves and their motivation is influenced, stimulated and shaped by their environment. Investigate any potential professional or personal issues, or the plausibility that any one or a combination of the three listed above can impact mindset.

The harder coaching assignment is when a manager perceives the issue to be one of motivation. Managers will often want to motivate their team. And they may have the very best of intentions, but the challenge is not your words or manner or even intent. The challenge is the listener is the one with the power to decide and act. Motivation is behaviors that people choose for themselves. To hear this may lead you to feel powerless. So you must change your thinking. You must move from "trying to motivate them" to "influencing and stimulating their motivation".

Whether it is contests or spiffs, managers use these tactics to motivate workers in a prescribed manner. This may influence short term results, but does not mean this one size fits all approach will cause long term sustainability. While short terms gains will always be a reality, we must move beyond this culture of entitlement and belief that work is only an economic transaction. The question changes from "How can I motivate others?" to "How can we create the conditions with which people motivate themselves?" This is not merely a philosophical question. It implies managers must look at the alternatives to stimulate and influence choice.

Vince Lombardi stated "Coaches who can outline plays on a black board are a dime a dozen. The ones who win get inside their player and motivate." Our next step is to engage in exploring best practices to assure proper coaching alignment.

Coaching is complicated because it can be many things at any and all times. Coaching is part of performance management. It is on the fly, on the floor and in real time. It is established formal one-on-one and team meetings. It is the way you conduct yourself at all times. It is general interaction, communication, mentoring, role-playing and the sharing of best practices. It can be just telling someone they just did a good job and you are proud of them. Regardless of the methodology, it does have some essentials.

Knowledge is first. This implies you know the critical three things when coaching. You must know your job "backwards and forwards" in order to provide meaningful feedback and insight. You must know the business and the KPI's by which it is measured. You must know what makes your team tick, especially what may be driving behavior and their individual needs. As a side note, this can be difficult if the team is constantly changing. Regardless the goal will always be to get to know your team.

You cannot deliver an effective coaching action plan without your observation. Great coaches know their game. They study previous games on film. They study the plays and the players' strengths and weaknesses. Imagine if that was all they did. The great coaches do all that and coach in real time on the sideline. Managers must temper their coaching with proportionate time on the floor. By seeing what happened, you then have a basis of understanding of what to coach; especially as it aligns with the KPI's.

A review must happen in three distinct parts. One is the actual review process. It is the tracking, compilation and analysis of performance. It is also the alignment of the behavioral cause to the statistical result. The next is the coaching review of the action plan with the team member. The key here is to always align a behavioral cause with a performance effect. Lastly, be sure to clarify the desired behavior and specific action with a numerical target and time frame for completion. Verify and ensure both parties are on the same page. Both need to provide a commitment.

Coaching is only as powerful as the results it creates. It must have a follow-up session to gauge both results as well as accuracy of coaching targets. Managers may find the coaching was inaccurate resulting in continued deficient performance. If behavior continues, you may need to re-discover or re-align root cause with a new action plan. Also, be sure to follow up with all types of coaching, like appraisal, feedback, praise, recognition, reward and, as needed, corrective action. Follow up exemplifies accountability to the job.

In addition, there are certain rules of engagement when creating structure behind your coaching efforts. It models the concept of using important increments. However, like all rules, they must be flexible due to the individual team member and the context.

For example, your approach would flex if someone has done extremely well versus someone who has been consistently struggling with hitting their numbers. Coaching is always unique to the situation and yet coaching must still have some type of a foundational structure. In addition, do not be so rigid that you make coaching, say exactly five minutes. The idea is to understand a balance within coaching.

Another consideration with coaching is the balance of positive to negative. Most coaching given is based on the intention of fixing something. It implies something is broken and needs to be corrected. If negative is all you hear, you become deaf. If praise is all you hear, you become static or apathetic. So which is the best balance? Make giving positive feedback more prevalent than negative feedback. The second part of this consideration is does rewarding performance cost more money? While what kind of rewards may be the first thing that comes to mind, it doesn't have to be a thing or cost a lot of money. Studies show a highly appreciated reward is a simple verbal "thank you" and written "thank you".

In closing, consider how re-orienting your mindset and embracing causality as an easier or more effective way to help others grow and develop. All coaching must first have a stimulus to coach, an understanding of what is behind the behavior and then a customized approach to influence motivation.

Activities

Reflection: Imagine one of your coaches in life. Describe their characteristics. Why did you choose that characteristic? Now describe your own coaching characteristics.

Reflection: What have been your excuses for not coaching, developing or giving feedback?

Exercise & Discussion: Make a list of the most common coaching situations you have faced with your team. Exchange the list with another manager and discuss what you would do.

Role-Play: Pick roles and work through the following situations:

- *Mary has been doing her share over and above. You appreciate all that she does. You catch her during some down time and want to her thank you for mentoring the new team members.*

Activities

- *You are really contemplating letting Chloe go. She has been on staff for 6 months and your fathers are best friends. You are really struggling if she can and will improve; one more chance?*

- *Todd drives you nuts; he is so loud and obnoxious. His performance is average and at times above average. You catch up with at the end of the day and ask why he has been so angry. You know he will completely overreact.*

- *Max is so shy and you really want him to "step up" and take a more visible approach to in his abilities, especially when interacting with the team. He is a nice guy, but takes feedback very negatively. You catch him after lunch and want to have a touch base.*

Now discuss what types of context play a part in these situations and what needs to be defined and clarified to make these situations effectively coach-able.

We do not see things as they are but as we are.
- Saying from the Talmud

12

Face

Who works for you? They each have a face. Today's workforce is the most unique in the history of mankind. Never before has there been so much diversity, and in so many ways. Think of your own business point of view. There lies a mix of gender, ethnicity and especially generation. Each has their own idiosyncrasies, as well their own unique strengths and challenges. Welcome to the global marketplace.

Research suggests we can now no longer manage others in the same ways we have, even in our most recent past. Our landscape is changing that significantly. When my dad instructed me and offered insight into working within his company during a summer position, I listened very intently. He is an awesome role model when it comes to a work ethic. He is widely respected for his integrity and "always get it done" attitude. I even remember my foremen remarking, "So you are Jim's son", as if to immediately establish some type of expectation. It did. Is my ethic yours? Is the way I look at and perceive a job well done the same as yours? No! This is at the heart of this chapter.

This chapter will first look deeper into a concept introduced in *Communication*, the Filter. How did you come to be who you are? One might say God had you planned from the beginning and another may say mom and dad. Regardless of which direction you lead, they are both right and include so many other things. Everything from your beliefs, relationships, education, family, personal and professional experiences shapes what makes you "you".

A filter is used to make decisions, to come to conclusions, to process data and to render judgment. This represents a memory mechanism which shapes your view of the world and your decisions within it. If it were to be drawn, it might look like a ring around your head. All information coming in and going out is distilled by this ring. Things in your life add structure and meaning to this ring. Remember when you were that one age and that certain thing happened. This event formed a value or belief which affects how you embrace new instances in your life. Even the smallest of things can influence how we make decisions in our life. This is what makes interacting with others both exciting and completely frustrating. It is frustrating because we all strive for control in all things. Lack of control can sound like, "I just don't get you" or "If I don't know what is feeding your perception, I cannot help you."

All too often we think managing others is just assigning tasks. It is based on our scope of understanding, preferred approach and how we would complete a task. We may assume and presume how people want direction and information. The equation is realizing the real truth in getting things done through others is an earnest desire for understanding others before asking them to perform anything. This is a monumental skill missed in preparing managers and leaders in general. We focus on the task, not the team member and their needs. Some managers are under the impression that we have to speak loudly or with great authority. The best leaders are those who appreciate and empathize with those they lead. They find out what the team needs individually. Some of the best conversations have more questions than statements in them. The questions are designed to better understand the individual or group's filter. The problem is if we don't ask, we simply fill in the blanks. It is time to stop guessing. If you only ask the questions, you will find better understanding.

Think of your team and how their filter impacts every interaction you have with them. Consider what you would need to ask to better know them and how they prefer to be managed or lead. There will be no complex methodology, ask your team questions. Ask yourself and create an inventory. Then, ask your team. This may be done in person or given as an assignment. Create a guide with a targeted questions in an effort to share insight into how people think, feel and what they need.

The action plan must allow a manager to be current, balanced and real, as well as consistent and focused. The role of manager is about being sensitive, yes. It is also about accountability. So be safe, just hire people like you. Just hire the right "them". Who is "them" exactly? As manager, you will always inherently be the boss or the supervisor or the big kahuna. You will definitely be diverse. That is the reality of being management today. You may also ask yourself, why? Someone felt you had merit in this position. You are worthy. It is just you are questioning the quality of your team. They are just a group of people who are looking for direction, leadership and inspiration.

Do you have to be the leader all the time every day? No, more times than not, your team is looking for you to share a simple "what" or "why" or "how" or "to what extent" in everything they embrace. I think back to my days as manager and remember a day when I was freaking out over a project and its due date. I was absolutely presenting an image of someone out of control. One of my team came up and said "OK, you need to relax". At that point, I realized what I was televising, what I was projecting to the team. Sometimes they are not the issue. It is you. More times than not, they are simply a reflection of you.

This is not to say the team is not at fault sometimes. It is to suggest, we need to stop and consider the real issue or the root cause within the members of your team. It is about how you allow yourself to be one who understands versus a desire to be understood. Business today is having a changing of the generational guard. One thing is the movement of Baby Boomers into retirement. Another is the significant global perspective to both employment and employers. The last thing is business is becoming increasingly more diverse across all lines. Bottom line, in any business, change and evolution is inevitable with team members having immense value with something significant to offer.

Generations in the workplace are a constant and sizeable consideration for employers. Mostly the issue is about who they are. It is our issue not automatically theirs. It is that simple and it is that hard at the same time. There are multiple books which provide the world with tremendous insight into the generations, their characteristics and, more importantly, how to work with them. As a means to provide valuable best practices, review this section and then research as much as possible.

The following represents general facts from a the book *Generations at Work: Managing the Clash of Veterans, Boomers, Xers, and Nexters in Your Workplace* by Ron Zemke, Claire Raines and Bob Filipczak:

Baby Boomers represent those born from 1943-1960 and are at about 73.2 million people. They were born during or after World War II and raised in the era of extreme optimism, opportunity, and progress.

Generation Xers were born from 1960-1980 and represent about 70.1 million people. This group was born of the Baby Boomers and excelled at getting things done as quickly and easily as possible. They began to interact in the workplace with the mentality, "what's in it for me?"

Nexters (or Millennials or Generation Y) were born from 1980 to 2000 and represent about 69.7 million people. They have been born of the late Baby Boomers and early Xers. They inherited our current high-tech landscape with "soccer-mom" support and "you can do anything" optimism.

I have found in the field, the issue is not the generation itself. It is however one's viewpoint that their generation somehow has it all figured out versus another. This is what creates the "they just don't get it" or "they just don't have a work ethic" mentality. They do. It just isn't your viewpoint. I have come to the conclusion; they will work just as hard as anyone else as long as we customize our approach to managing and leading one another based on what is important to them.

Gender is something else to pay attention to. It will always require more information than what may be discussed in just this book. Again do your research in addition to anything you might read. Here is why. I will never forget an evaluation from one of my learners after a workshop. She said she was offended I discussed and even mentioned a gender dynamic to management. At first, I felt bad and went into a review of what I might have said to encourage a response. Then I realized while sitting in the airport. Yeah, there is something to consider and new managers need to be aware of what might be part of the equation of gender.

Maybe the better thing is to express the importance of an awareness of how gender is perceived. If you are a woman reading this, you might ask "why is this author the right person to speak about this?"

Here is why I say this. I do not have a doctorate in this topic. Therefore I might be immediately dismissed. So here we go. Women are different then men. There, I said it. Does that make me a bigot? I am not espousing that a woman or a man is any better than the other to manage, lead, inspire, direct or influence others. In fact, if you know me, you would know the best manager in my frame of reference is my wife. So what is my point? The difference is we must create a basis for understanding apart from gender. It must be based on what is important to each of us as individuals.

The pivotal point in our history was the migration of women into the professional landscape during World War Two. Seven million women left their homes and families to support the war effort. What a tremendous moment. And yet, even after the seventy years which have passed, men still do not get it. Women still work very hard at their place at the table; despite some knucklehead men who cannot or will not embrace this wonderful diversity.

Women may worry about being respected for their opinions. Picture a group of managers. They are peers. A woman and man state the same point. Who would be considered first as the subject matter expert? Men may worry about possible confusion as it pertains to the ground rules regarding the sexes. Also, in a group of mixed team members, is a man assumed the boss? Does a woman who is focused on accountability treated differently than a man? Does gender decide the better mentor? There is significant research being done right now which suggests women are better at mentoring and developing others. Sexual harassment (with either gender) is a huge situation and one that requires greater understanding. The key is to understand what this actually is. Research this. This topic is way too big. Communication skills will always be reviewed. Many men recognize when they say something to a woman it is either heard differently or at least reacted upon differently. It shouldn't matter whether the receiver is a male or female, what you say, how you say it and the impact of the statement must always be considered.

Whether you are a man or woman, the key is to remain both authentic and respectful. Is that possible? I believe it is. I have spent over twenty years training and consulting groups of people and gender has never been an issue. My approach is one of you are part of an important whole, not a segregated bunch of folks. Treat each other with the same respect and with equal amount of value and worth. Get to know each other as a person first. Maybe it was my Midwest upbringing, I just think everyone is someone to get to know, embrace, listen to and celebrate. Think team first always.

The critical awareness needed by a manager regarding working with a team (not just about generation or gender) is a clear understanding of motivation. Managers will often want to motivate their team. This is the first issue to face. That in of itself is the root of confusion and disillusionment on the part of managers. Think about the last time you said, "They just don't get it." Are you sure? Or do you not get them?

Many managers have said to me, "I can motivate my people." You cannot motivate others. They motivate themselves. This was expressed in the previous chapter. This is the reality behind the face of your team. To hear this may lead you to feel powerless. So you must change your mindset. You must move from "trying to motivate your team" to "influencing and stimulating their motivation".

Consider the following. A client asks for a specific item by name. It is an item you normally have, but are not in stock at the present time. The team member has four choices, what are they?

- Switch the client (immediate and supportive of a specific need)

- Get what the client needs (may take time and involves a targeted desire)

- Send the client somewhere else (may mean you do not get the sale)

- Do nothing (this involves you doing nothing and letting them walk away)

What in turn motivates the team member to make the "right choice"? This is a huge question. This is motivation. If you and I would do one thing or another in a specific context, you must embrace what someone else might do in this same situation. Have you established a selection of best practices on how should certain things occur within the business? Your team will do what is perceived as the best plan of action based on their relative knowledge of the situation. Motivation is about choice. Managers must look to ways to influence decision making. If management is in fact a relationship, then it is a two-way street. This implies to have a goal of better understanding ourselves and each other. In this case, the goal would be to understand your decision making machine and the one of your team.

To conclude, you may never know the extent of one's filter or motivation. People will only allow so much information to be shared. Imagine a team member with an addiction of some type. Sounds heavy; it is. They may never share the extent of what motivates them and this thing may be a significant element within their filter. Can you manage that? You can as it aligns with their professional behavior on the job – that's it. Managers must know people do as people are and there are limits to what we can manage.

Activities

Reflection: Identify those characteristics which make up your filter.

Reflection: You are now in posture of authority over a team. Identify your next steps.

Discussion: Considering the following situations, identify the questions you might ask and courses of action you would take. Consider your team, their possible questions and their reactions.

- New program on accountability within the organization.
- A respected mentor was "let go".
- Training on Operations was deemed by your team as ineffective.
- Your best performer is in conflict with your substandard performer.
- You now have a supervisor no one respects.

Peer Discussion: Identify the characteristics of your generational work force.

Activities

Exercise: Have your team identify the responses to the following requests.

- List three things that give you energy when on the job.

- List three things that sap your energy when on the job.

- List three things that you want to achieve on the job.

Discussion: Identify the challenges you currently face regarding team diversity within your organization.

Group Discussion & Exercise: Set up groups of people based on their birth years 1943-1960, 1960-1980 and 1980-2000. First discuss how it feels to be segregated. Then, begin making a list of characteristics you as a group have collectively (perhaps unique to your time frame). Share this list with the others. Begin to look for common ground and how there is value within each group.

I not only use all the brains I have, but all that I can borrow.

- Woodrow Wilson

13

Collaboration

A sad truth is many team members today produce a series of events leading to a paycheck and that's it. What
else is there? In many cases what may be missing is an
understanding of the people around us. This knowledge or lack of knowledge may affect our production
and overall well-being in the workplace. Maybe it can
be a goal of connecting with others or at least an effort to better understand one another. This chapter
will look at the power of having degrees of common
understanding within your team. It will explore how
to create affinity to ensure productivity and efficiencies, and more than that, it will define ways to elevate
people and the overall team dynamic.

One of the most common rally cries from a manager is "Let's work as a team." Is that possible, truly? Any group of people, however much they may have in common with the same set of goals and objectives, will always gravitate towards what affects them individually. They arrive to work with their own motivations and drive to accomplish what matters most to them. Personal agendas and cliques get in the way of becoming one. Then add stress, change, diversity and turnover. Ultimately, too much gets in the way of becoming a team.

If teamwork is so elusive, what is the answer of bringing people together? Teamwork is a result. Causality, or cause-effect, is essential to better understand teamwork. What I do as a manager and leader will have an impact on a team. What I do to learn more and listen better to my co-workers will impact a team. What I do to establish and nurture relationships will impact a team.

This is not a search for team, but rather what needs to precede team. This is a search for common understanding of what impacts teamwork. If you break down teamwork to its root system, you will find affinity. This is not about how to like each other, that's tough. It is about what can be done to get to know one another, find some type of common ground and begin collaborating on the same page more often than not.

We start with affinity. Affinity is defined as a natural attraction, liking, or feeling of kinship and an inherent similarity between persons or things. A classic example of affinity is when parents will walk into a room with other parents and immediately have an understanding or connection with them. They understand what it is like to have children and to be out with them. It can be applied to many different situations. Imagine you are a passenger in a large line to check-in at the airport and someone cuts into the line. You all freak out. You share immediate common ground.

Think of that one co-worker. It is the team member that drives you crazy. Maybe they constantly crunch ice at their desk or you cannot stand their choice in shoes. Many times you will be at a meeting with that person, you will just look at them and be annoyed. Consider that you are forming a preconceived notion about that person. What would happen if you asked them about this feeling and found out they are that way because of something they think about you? We are quick to agree with this concept until we find out we are that annoying person to someone else.

The goal of affinity is to find ways, any way to connect with each other. Again, it is not necessarily about liking each other but rather an effort to find ways to create better fundamental relationships. Creating a balance of being understood and understanding others is critical to the goal of affinity. The ego wants to be understood, to be appreciated. It is self-serving. That is the challenge with affinity. You have to make an effort to understand others, despite a desire to be understood first. You have to take the time to ask questions. You have to take the time to listen. You have to take time for a little empathy.

The creation of a team dynamic must begin with a leader and their abilities to foster an environment of better understanding one another. If the manager is self-serving, it will become very apparent and affect everyone involved in the team. If the leader is narcissistic or a lover of self, will they really have the team's interests at heart? Use these questions as a talking point with both your peers and supervisors. Be careful and be honest.

There is a time and place when the manager and leader need to make decisions. Giving your team the ability to make their own decisions also has a time and place. In fact, I will always lean towards the opportunity of sharing possibilities versus the absolutism of "my way or the highway". Think of the last issue you faced. What and how did you decide? Did your decision impact others? Would the involvement of others make or have made an impact?

Consider the power relationship and ways to collaborate within it. Does that sound like a contradiction in terms? It does because collaboration potentially promotes an opposing viewpoint to a manager who must decide a plan of action. It suggests a goal of getting, hearing and listening to someone else's opinion. It involves having value for and in someone else.

The argument for a new collaborative environment begins with the task and the decision making, and more specifically the distance between. The team member is instructed to get a job done. The manager is required to oversee the task. Both parties understand the intricacies involved in the task but from different perspectives. One group may not know what may surround getting the task done and lack knowledge regarding the task. Another group may not have the big picture or why behind whatever the task may be.

What if the team member was given a share of the responsibility to decide upon and execute the targeted activities? What would happen to buy-in or the overall implementation? If people are valued for their roles, individual competencies, contributions and results within an organization, will it make a difference? Now, more than ever, we must be able to provide information to our people so that they can be prepared to be successful." Managers must become the coach of decision making rather than the main overseer of activity. This is at the heart of a collaborative environment.

This will be your decision before we start. Consideration of implementing a collaborative environment is a great beginning point. Do not rush to change too much within your organization. It will become apparent, even small collaborative tactics can and will influence not only your team's decision making, but also their desire to be part of the overall organization. These tactics can simply elevate a sense of teamwork.

Schedule collaboration as a habitual activity whereby you illicit your teams' input. It needs to be the right method for the exchange of data. The exchange process needs to be clearly defined. You must clarify the path of providing feedback, the distillation of what is provided and what will happen with the final information. Nothing is more frustrating than giving someone your thoughts and nothing happens. It needs to fit the organizational culture. The approach needs to match and be relevant with how people interact within the reality of your organization.

Collaboration is an easy behavior to instill, however the burden is living it and what you model may be potentially emulated behavior. The old adage "Do as I say, not as I do" cannot be the benchmark any longer for manager and leader behavior. Moreover, the generational aspect of the workforce is the main driver for this behavior. Studies suggest the new generational workforce (i.e. the "Nexters" or "Millennials") will need more cooperation and stimulation than their "Gen Xer" predecessors. The younger new entrants to the workplace will be looking for more attention and structure from the authority figure. For years American companies have espoused a need to treat team members as customers. It is time to make that a reality.

Supporting collaboration is perhaps most commonly missed; especially within the hierarchical management style of "because I said so." Being an authoritarian or micro-manager has tremendous reverberations in how people feel connected. Consider the mantra of train and trust. This implies the need for an educational engine which supports and develops your team. In addition, there must be a resource where within a safe environment, team members can experience the tasks, practice them and learn by trial and error. At the end, there must be engrained a release element whereby the expression of trust is given.

A big roadblock will be biases. In society, today, we have a tendency to put people in boxes, to create some kind of stereotype, all based on one or more biases. This behavior makes empathy a very difficult thing to achieve. A belief, whether justified or not, can influence how much or to what degree you embrace another. Maybe the guy or gal next to you has a different view or political ideology or religious belief, does it matter? It does. It does, because it matters to them. And if you are especially trying to better understand why someone is the way they are and what makes them "them", it matters. Here is the thing; you never have to agree with that view or political ideology or religious belief. You just have to understand it matters to them.

Lastly, do not confuse collaboration as being overly

sympathetic. When discussing team, we must isolate empathy as a best practice and clarify how this differs from sympathy. The simple difference is sympathy is about agreement and empathy is about understanding. If being sympathetic to an issue, you might say "You know what, you're absolutely right. It makes no sense to create that program." If being empathetic, you might say "I understand how this might be an issue. What are your thoughts as to why we shouldn't go forward?" So which is better? Both are good, given the circumstances. Conviction and goals will definitely play a part in which path may be the best one to follow.

Activities

Discussion: Think of a time you were on some type of team. This could sports-related or not. Identify those things that made the team, the team.

Discussion: Identify those things that keep you from getting to know others.

Discussion: Define your interpretation of collaboration. Define how collaboration is perceived within your organization.

Exercise: Consider a goal or objective, either currently in place or being planned. Begin making notes on how you can adopt a collaborative environment with your team regarding the goal.

- Considering the state of your organization, identify ways you can schedule collaborative activities.

- Identify ways you can model behavior.

- Identify ways you can better express and support the goal.

Activities

Exercise: Interviewing each other...
Pair up with someone and ask them to provide the following information.

- Life changes
- Background Events
- Goals

Exercise: Personal Skills, Professional Skills, Technical Skills.

Part One: List your skills in all three categories.

Part Two: Find at least one useful similarity and one useful difference with others in your group. Focus on the word "useful".

Part Three: Identify what skills in these three categories can be useful to you personally, professionally, and technically. Discuss how you apply these to working effectively with each other.

Improved listening skills will not necessarily result in improved listening. We must apply these skills. We must be convinced that it pays to listen. The combination of desire (I want to listen), effort (I'm going to work at it), and skill (I know how to do it) will result in improved listening.

– Donald Kirkpatrick

14

Training

What comes to mind when you hear the word training? To be perfectly frank, while this is my profession, I believe training has a bad taste for some people. Either they have had a poor trainer-facilitator who read reams of content or they had someone or something which did not provide relevance or immediate practicality.

This has been a huge focus for me and my clients recently. An owner or senior leader says they need training and call someone like me. I create the event. The learners enjoy the day or days. They are inspired. Simply put, they get trained on something, so what? Perhaps another way to look at it is they were provided training and inspired to create change. So what happened? Is it any wonder people have a bad taste with training? Regardless, there will still be the questions like why do it in the first place, what is the desired objective, what is being targeted for improvement and what were the results?

I subscribe to the theory put forth by a professor emeritus at the University of Wisconsin. His name is Dr. Donald Kirkpatrick. In 1959, he published his theory on the evaluation of training programs. In many ways, it is considered the most highly influential model for training evaluation. It consists of four levels: Reaction, Learning, Behavior and Results.

Briefly, reaction is the job of the trainer. The facilitation (in whatever form) must create a reaction or response within the learner to identify a need, a why. Learning is the responsibility of the learner in a way. The response they have must align itself with a desired next step on what they learned and retained. This is what must happen next. Behavior is the drilling down to how the learning takes shape. It is the aspects of the learning which must be replicate-able, do-able and relevant to the need. Results are the big one. Has this effort stuck? How do you know and to what extent has this behavior been adopted?

Some authors interject a fifth element – return on investment. This is significant, especially if you wrote the check. In a 2008 Wall Street Journal article, Dr. Harry J. Martin of Cleveland State University stated, "Teaching team members new skills is one thing. Getting them to apply what they have learned is quite another." He went on to suggest, "With some studies suggesting that 10 to 40 percent of training is ever used on the job, it is clear that a big chunk of the tens of billions of dollars organizations spend annually on staff development is going down the drain."

This chapter is designed to clarify two things; to look at how information is shared with learners to impact retention and what does the information need to do as it leads to adoption. One element of this section may be a realization of what was done, period – good or bad. The other is not to be critical in the end but progressive in making your organization more effective and efficient in its training (statistical or behavioral change) management.

Consider this debate – education versus training. Is there a difference? I recently discussed this with a respected colleague. He posed this question and I had fun thinking about this. I think there is. We both agreed education is about learning something. It can be and usually is a very academic approach. In a way, it is about a better understanding of a thing, concept, topic, etc. Training, on the other hand, is (and should be) about taking the learning and applying it. It is the "how to do it and how to apply it" part. How many times have you been in a training and the time spent was only educating you on something without the "how to do it" part? Does this mean training cannot include education? No. It does suggest that "doing-ness" has got to be the larger part of "knowing-ness" in order for training to be effective.

In addition to this debate is the realization that even after training, there needs to be something else in place to sustain and adopt ongoing reinforcement and growth. What are the steps? Is that not the question new managers ask?

First, let's explore what helps retention. What does training look like and which method works best and why? Many times, organizations do what they think is the best financially – cut training or make it more logistically accessible. Money may dictate learning. E-learning or some type of Learning Management System (LMS) becomes the only mode of learning. I do not disagree with this type of learning. It has tremendous value, but not as the stand alone process of learning. What is missing by many is the understanding of what helps people learn is to invest in all types of learning as a blended approach to support retention and adoption.

Every organization must define its training methodology as it aligns with its training culture.

Training others can be very difficult. This simplified statement is meant to set a stage for the biggest element and consideration of a training session. What did they learn or retain? Some studies state that as little as 10 percent is retained by a learner within any training session (the average can be seen as about 25 percent; again in general). Here is the twenty-five thousand dollar question, is it the right, consistent or at least your desired 10 to 25 percent?

Research show people learn best in chunks, or small targeted amounts. The most common mistake is to force as much as possible in the time scheduled. Giving too much data is as detrimental as giving too little. Training is like a filling a glass of water. You have to let the learner drink or the glass will overflow. Break down your training into five chunks; plus or minus two. Lay out your training objectives in logical sequence, especially if one skill is dependent on another. Ensure your training has a clearly defined "what", "why", "how" and "to what extent". And practice is key - a lot of practice. Make content second to the experiential part of learning.

Individuals learn differently. A number of things like experience, background and aptitude all influence how we learn. Our instinct is to suggest we learn better one way versus another; however, we effectively learn

by each. In fact, we can learn by all of them simultaneously. Ultimately, the most effective style depends
more on the topic than the individual preference. Although learners may all have tendencies or preferences
towards a particular style; review the topic or environment beforehand to ensure the best style for learning.
The best approach is to use a balance of all six.

Visual highlights the use of visual stimuli. The entails the use of pictures, movies, graphs, colors, or having something physical to view.

Auditory is what you hear. Therefore the goal is
eliminate as many distractions as possible to enable listeners to focus on what is being said or heard.

Kinesthetic promotes the engagement of activities.
This entails participation in role-playing, exercises,
games or problem solving.

Collaborative represents people that learn best with
others around or as a collective. It can be the sharing of
best practices or working a situation together to come
to a group consensus.

Linear relates to a learning model which has a
particular flow or logical sequence. In other words, a
learner will need to hear what comes first before moving onto the next thing.

Contextual is about a story or analogy. This style of learning is about having something presented in a relative context in order to best learn the objective. For example, telling a story about a personal sales experience to highlight what to do or not to do.

Studies show time and time again, adults learn effectively through practice. In fact, adult learning must be more experiential than content-oriented. It is certainly best if you have a safe environment with the allowance for mistakes to be made through practice. The use of simulations, role-plays and "what if" situations help your team problem solve and explore all the possible solutions in their job. These activities can minimize the amount of mistakes made on the job. Make the practice challenging. Would you rather they practice on your customers? Practicing the easy stuff is easy; work the difficult side of the training. Don't just do it once; try it again and again. Change the scenario and work it again.

Reoccurring feedback states, the best part of learning or perhaps the most appreciated, was the portion that allowed for peer-to-peer discussion and group problem-solving. This is collaboration. While the fear may be the information shared between learners or their best practices may be flawed, it allows for an open forum. This is always makes for a positive environment. You must be in charge to ensure all discussions stay on track and on task. Initiate a topic and let the learners answer – even if there is uncomfortable silence at first. Be sure to ensure best practices are in alignment with learning and bridge as needed.

Effective training is linked to a specific business problem or issue with a practical and immediate application when the session ends. Have you ever been to a training session and asked yourself, "What was the point?" Let that fuel your training mindset. Nothing builds confidence in a team member more than something that is both relevant and achievable. Remember, your credibility impacts the training. You must clarify the relationships between training objectives and the applicable behaviors. Provide relative case studies, research and real-life results.

Now adoption is the focus. This is the FU Stage (the follow-up stage). After the training takes place, it is the simple practice of checking understanding as well as if the team is adopting the training objectives. This is perhaps the most critical aspect of training. Use simulations, role-plays and exercises to gauge learning. Encourage your team to teach back the information. Do not make this a condescending event. Your goal is to ensure your communication effectiveness and support their clarity of expectations. One aspect is immediate follow-up. Then there is long term follow-up.

As a facilitator for more than twenty years, I would boldly and fervently state, that while curriculum design and facilitation is important, it is the call to action and a clearly defined next step which matters most. What makes the training powerful is to define and support the big questions at the end of any training session; like "OK, so what do you want me to do tomorrow?" This represents where we find ourselves after training. It is important to start here first to ensure the training has a clear and defined message. Training sets a stage, and businesses must assess themselves at getting a message across to a team. It is one thing to be present and understand training. It is another to replicate its impact.

At some point, you will be done training a specific skill and the team will be accountable for the training they have received. The most common reason training falls short is a lack of follow-up. Specifically, a lack of a well-defined, structured follow-up agenda. The situation will always be how to justify the resources spent on training and will you notice your efforts has equaled or exceeded expectation? If this is the problem after a training session, all efforts must then require follow up. The fix is to extend efforts beyond the training. It must involve follow-up activities such as peer meetings and performance assessments. It must clarify measurement and the review of the current state of implementation.

Basic question; how many times have you trained a group and then that was the last time you covered the topic? Your team will expect some type of effort on your part to ensure they are on track. This represents observation, coaching and measurement. This is follow up. When possible, provide feedback immediately following the behavior. When providing feedback, be specific on the behavior. The closer you place the feedback to the behavior, the more likely the recipient will correlate the feedback to the desired or targeted behavior. Ask the team member what they saw or for their perception of how they handled a situation. For example, ask "How do you feel about your performance? What would you do differently?" Schedule an ongoing and regular review of performance based on observation and analysis.

Another way to reinforce training is to measure its impact. Every initiative you implement must relate to some type of indicator being measured. This may simply represent the tracking of various and targeted sales and productivity metrics. It could show up on POS reports or any manually tracked compliance reports. When positioning a value-based proposition in the market place, you begin to look towards how the overall experience measures up. So whether you use a family member or vendor resource, a mystery shop will allow you to see what type of service you create. Remember, do not get hung up on the minutiae of one visit, analyze overall findings and trend. When in doubt, ask a team member or client. The insight into either (or both) may identify not only the return on investment, but also future training opportunities.

Another option is to create a performance assessment. The goal is to measure specific behaviors targeted by the training. The assessment may include evaluations, survey ratings, operational cost savings, return on sales and reduction in errors. This tactic increases motivation to use skills due to observation and feedback on performance, monitors and evaluates proficiencies and allows others to provide peripheral feedback to gauge cross-departmental perspective.

This is simple, is the team "talking about it"? If you do not hear rumblings, that may be a bad thing. Think about the last big change you went through. I bet you connected with your group or peers and talked it up big time. Imagine if no one said anything. Imagine if your team said nothing about something you delivered with passion.

Activities

Discussion: What does training look like in your organization?

Exercise: Create an inventory of action items within a recent training; esp. exploring what was to be accomplished. List each training activity and note its current status.

Exercise: You are planning a session on "Engaging the Customer" or "Dealing with Difficult Customers". Considering the best practices, how would you construct your training session?

Activities

Exercise: List all activities which may assist both retention and adoption.

RETENTION: This applies to two aspects of
how the training created impact: "What was
learned" and "What stuck". Stickiness becomes a
very important word after any training session.

ADOPTION: This is where learning turns into
doing. Consider the saying, "we all know what
to do, but we don't always do what we know."
Senior leaders become very happy when training
turns into increased performance.

You can have brilliant ideas, but if you can't get them across, your ideas will not get you anywhere.

– Lee Iacocca

15

Meetings

One of the essential communication responsibilities in management is holding meetings. Although you may be fearful of public speaking, you are not trying to win any awards, only inform. That is your mindset; "How can I ensure my team knows precisely what I need them to know?"

Fear of public speaking is called *glossophobia* (or, in-formally, "stage fright"). It is believed to be the single most common phobia – affecting as much as 75 per-cent of the population. Fear of oration ranks higher than death. Many careers require some ability in public speaking, for example presenting information to cus-tomers or colleagues.

At one time or another we have to say something, somewhere. You will find yourself in a place having to present a thought or collection of thoughts to a group of people who may or may not have the knowledge or context of what is being shared. They may also not care what you have to say. This is both the reality and challenge with what needs to happen next. How would you rate?

This chapter is designed to aid those who know they must communicate to others and are challenged with the best practices in not only getting their point across, but also in a way that compels those same others into action.

If you don't clarify the direction for your team, they will clarify it for you. Understand the importance of what that statement means to both you and the re-ceiver within the meeting. "Tell them what you are going to tell them, tell them, and then tell them what you told them."

Preparation is critical in most things in life. You can use the analogy of sports and how the preparation before the game allows you to hone your skills. Maybe you believe in Einstein's statement that, "imagination is more important than knowledge" or that being improvisational and thinking on your feet is a more organic approach. Whichever may be your philosophy; do you know the intent of what you will speak about, the people who will be listening and the cause-effect it is intended to create?

What do you feel when you have to stand in front of a group of people? I remember my first time standing in front of people. It was a training session on product knowledge. The goal was to share my insight into how knowledge about the product would help them sell more. I looked out at the different people. Some had been around for a while and some had just shown up. I knew my stuff and I had to adapt at several occasions to help everyone learn. I was prepared, imaginative and improvisational.

Let's make it easy. Know what you are going to say. Understand that what you will say may be interpreted by different degrees or gradients of understanding. This is first and key. Spend time thinking about all the perspectives you may have in the group. This becomes easier when it is just a small group, your team. It doesn't make it less important, only a bit easier to relate to those you manage and lead. Think about the following:

KNOWLEDGE OF TOPIC

What is the topic mean?

What are the learning objectives?

What words or phrases will be important to the topic?

What are the particulars regarding the topic?

KNOWLEDGE OF AUDIENCE

Who makes up the audience?

What their needs regarding the topic?

What is the best way to get the message across?

How will the presentation affect their learning?

KNOWLEDGE OF CAUSALITY

What is the end-result of the topic?

How will the particulars impact the audience (Think WIIFM)?

What is it specifically you want the audience to do tomorrow?

How will the impact be seen and/or measured?

How will everyone know their score and how they individually performed?

Every meeting you ever conduct needs to be built on some type of foundation. It is these consistencies that help you develop your skills and establish behaviors. Having a foundation does not mean you cannot ad lib or be improvisational. Quite the contrary, having the foundation allows you to be more or immediately flexible and adaptive.

Be sure to have a point. Meetings require a reason for being; the audience expects to know what it is you want to them to do, precisely and without ambiguity. Credibility is the by-product of having a plan and executing it. Consider the old saying, "Keep it simple". Do not over complicate your message or direction. More importantly, be sure you not only have a clear goal or set of goals, but ensure what you say matches the specific behaviors you expect. Before your meeting, run a pre-check to ensure you have your agenda, notes, key thoughts or stories to share. Remember, people learn best with 3-5 chunks of information. Think like your audience and be prepared to answer their question; "What is it exactly you need to me to do tomorrow?"

All meetings must be organized. The logistics of "what, when, how long, and who" need to be clearly defined. Be sure to plan ahead for your meetings; not only for your benefit, but also for the benefit of your team. The best meetings are those that your team expects. And lastly, start all meetings on time. If you start late for this meeting, you send a message it is OK to start late for anything. Be proactive; let the team know ahead of time regarding the key elements to be covered. Focus on Topics, Goals/Objectives, Highlights, Next Steps and Follow Up. Consider the use of some type of structured meeting planner. Make sure those attending have the agenda at least 24 hours before the meeting. Remind all participants to be prepared for interaction and collaboration. You may even want to assign pre-work before the meeting.

The best meetings are the ones where everyone is involved. This would be everything from asking questions, simulations, role-plays, exercises, and small group discussion. Involvement means you care not only for their input and collaboration, but their accountability to being present as well. Always have questions ready to ask group. Stimulate the discussion with the types of questions that force people to reflect. Think of opportunities to create games in the meeting. This will simulate the competition found inherently in all people. You will see characteristics of how they perform by how they play the game. At different times, assign parts of the meeting to designated team members; based either on their abilities or your delegation.

Meetings require control in order to stay on track. Preparation establishes this. It is critical your team understand what is expected of them during the meeting. For example, if you want their feedback or opinions, set it up accordingly. If you want to stay on track and minimize feedback, then explain that at the very beginning. If you notice a movement in a direction away from your meeting objectives; either table it for discussion in a future meeting or immediately following the current meeting with all key players.

Accountability will always start and end with you. It begins with your ability to be the expert of whatever topic you choose, or at a minimum, the conduit for an SME (Subject Matter Expert) leading the meeting. It exists in how you ensure everyone both understands the goals as well as how to conduct their behaviors. Also, you are the one who holds everyone accountable after the meeting. You decide what is and what is not negotiable. Set all expectations at the very beginning; for example, turning off phones, time frame, when questions should be asked, and targeted learning objectives. Stay on topic. Be consistent with your meeting behavior.

Nothing is more frustrating to a meeting presenter than someone leaving the meeting without a clear understanding of what is expected. The purpose of your meeting is to inform and ensure understanding. Avoid having to have the same conversation twice by checking understanding at various times throughout the meeting. If you are having to re-explain or re-do a task, create more time by simply asking "Do you understand?" and then follow up with "OK, now teach me." Check understanding by some the following means: teach backs, role-plays problem solving, simulations, direct questions and application of skill exercises. If you think it is confrontational to ask for their understanding, soften the question by saying "I ask this to ensure I am communicating effectively."

Simple, people are drawn to enthusiasm. Your team relies on you for direction regarding sales and productivity as well as the energy and vibe within the store. Fun and discipline are not exclusive of one another. What is your "A" game? Be yourself. Showing passion does not mean being happy at all costs. It does mean believing in what you are saying – people can read insincerity. Select communication behaviors include making eye contact, using varying tone and inflection, practicing bold body movement and gesturing (as long as it is characteristic and not campy), and smiling when it is appropriate.

This is a consistent and important question asked by all managers, "What is the best time frame for a meeting?" It depends. It depends on the nature of the meeting, the logistics, the audience and many other things. Therefore, it will be difficult to specify a best time frame. Whatever length you choose, here are some adult learning considerations.

45 minutes is an average threshold for sitting in any meeting. This does not mean anything longer is inherently dangerous. It does mean the flow of your meeting, like taking breaks must factor into consid-

eration. It may mean you will need to do something different, or change gears, or create a creative learning exercise to redirect the flow. Learners need to do something physical every 20 to 25 minutes. Like the comments above, something needs to happen to get learners engaged in activity. It could be an exercise, role-play, brainstorming session, etc.

As far as the frequency of your meetings, they all are different with different intentions. Due to the immediacy of the business, a type of quick daily meeting or "Huddle" is designed for those impromptu meetings which are less formal and time intensive. This sets the tone of the day by reviewing the daily targets and yesterday's results. Ideally this is for the occasions when at a moment's notice you can immediately influence activity and behavior. The targeted pockets of time could be before the day starts, during shift changes, down time during operational hours or as a days end review. Keep them short; five to ten minutes.

Weekly is the traditional one-on-one dynamic. It allows and establishes a regular time to review results and proactive goals. Many times it is best to make this meeting mandatory with a specific day and time. What is noticed most by the team member is that they have a special time to meet with their leader. It also aligns activities and coaching in a reasonable time to affect a month's productivity. Doing this as a bi-weekly event is also a consideration. No more than ten minutes.

Monthly is the traditional group meeting. This is what most managers think of when they think "meeting". The format typically holds multiple topics and held onsite or offsite to review month-end results and new goals. A big new goal must be to make the meeting highly collaborative. One to two hours is sufficient. If longer, ensure there are many designed moments for interaction and sharing of ideas.

While Quarterly is designed to review performance, celebrate accomplishments, and review results, it must also share strategic vision. This is your opportunity to help keep your team plugged into a bigger picture. The most successful buy-in is created by being part of the process and decision making. Again, one to two hours is sufficient.

Activities

Exercise: Create a one-page document to assist you through any meeting, regardless of length, and be able to highlight all elements at a simple glance. It must consist of but not be limited to the following fields:

- Logistics; like date time and location.

- Topic(s); by designating the focus for the meeting .

- Goal(s); by writing down the clear and precise goals of the meeting and what you plan to accomplish.

- Meeting Highlights; by writing down your key points with supporting data and questions for group to either stimulate discussion or check understanding.

- Next Step(s); by identifying any specific items to complete after the meeting with targets and timelines.

- Follow Up; by Identifying any/all control measures to ensure implementation.

Discussion: Think the topic for an upcoming meeting. Now proactively consider all possible questions from your team.

Exercise: Consider the following topics and identify what would be important to include in the meeting to ensure understanding, clarity and buy-in:

- Sales/Service
- Product Knowledge
- Policy/Procedure
- Operations
- Contest/Incentive
- Promotion
- Brainstorming

Part 4: CHOICE

People don't resist change, they resist being changed.

- Peter Scholtes

16

Change

Like *Communication*, change is a vast topic and in all aspects of life. Change and business are incredibly linked, from the rapid development of technology to the complexity of customer demographics to the growth and evolution of the market place. When change occurs, your team will not magically start doing it. As manager, you have to manage both the understanding and implementation of change.

Experience and countless case studies have shown change management is dynamic and continuous. It not only affects you at the point of implementation, but also will affect you later. Do not expect to maintain the perfect map you draw. Managing strategic change begins with you knowing there will be give-and-take and a need for flexibility all along the way.

For example, you decide to adapt a customer service step to include a one-month follow-up call to ensure client satisfaction. This could be a big change for your business with your goal of impacting client loyalty and retention. You feel you have carefully thought it through and believe you have planned accordingly. Be prepared for getting buy-in from team, it not happening quickly enough, the team not telling you they don't understand, figuring out how to measure impact and success and all the other issues taking precedence at the exact time.

The key to change is buy-in, which means allowing your team to have a voice and then allowing yourself to listen to it. Creating change is related to getting buy-in. The argument can be made that getting someone's buy in involves a deliberate act of selling a cause. The goal should be creating an environment whereby people are stimulated and allowed to have a say and in unison with others towards a common cause.

The main thing in making buy-in successful is to not overcomplicate what you are trying to accomplish. Keep it simple. More than that, whatever you are trying to do must also be easy to understand and the "why" behind it crystal clear. Think of the word *core*. This is what is at the heart of what you are trying to accomplish. One might say it is the root cause or ultimate reason of being. For example, "I need to implement a new sales process. It will have very specific behavioral expectations." What is at the core of this new initiative? Is it to drive sales productivity, increase levels of customer service, ensure a heighten sense of accountability or influence the team's ability to make more money?

Without clearly identifying the core of the initiative, it will suffer interpretation based on the relative understanding of those engaged in the action. Without sharing the core with your team, it may be very difficult for them to have affinity or common ground with what you are trying to accomplish. Therefore communication represents a huge opportunity – how do we communicate the core more effectively? It is one thing to know the core. It is another to communicate it. Therefore, we must look at communication as the first step in working with change.

People rarely embrace change positively when they are told to do something. On the other hand, if people are aware of the context for change, they may very well be more willing to engage change. One of the best ways to create context is to share a story or use an analogy for the basis of the change. The story is most effective when it reinforces the core. For example, regarding the new sales process, share a story about a personal experience with poor salesmanship.

Do not hide facts within the change, be transparent. Let your team know the what, why, how and to what extent. In addition, tell them what will happen, what may happen and what to do if something does not happen. Be upfront and proactive. For example, do not just explain the new sales process, plan to communicate what why, how and to what extent, as well as the "WIIFM" (What's in it for me) and "WIIFU" (What's in it for us)" and the "What If's".

It is impossible to over-communicate a goal or core value; especially if it is meaningful and relevant. There is not a magic number, just more than just once. The importance of making change stick will dictate the number. The more you reinforce the core, the more your team will be part of the adoption of change. Make follow up obvious. For example, make the new sales process a daily topic and continually share updates on the how the implementation is progressing.

Collaboration and brainstorming represent the act of providing a forum for your team to offer their thoughts, ideas and even fears. When you are implementing a new change within your organization, do not start your first meeting by telling your team what needs to be done. Give them the quick review and then ask them their "why" regarding this change and "how" it should be done. For example, position the new sales process and then have the team share their ideas for completing the new change, potential challenges, and requirements for reinforcement and recognition.

Openness (this keeps coming up) can be a hard one to adopt. The best leaders and managers listen to their team. This is easier said than done. This must begin as a determined mindset to always be growing yourself while working towards growing others. For example, allow the team to teach you about the possibilities of the new sales process. This may require you to be very direct in asking for their opinions and feedback. Then, you must listen. You may also want to elect someone to take notes for review.

Training is the most sought after and illusive concept. Sought after because every company knows it is necessary and illusive because managers struggle with the best method to accomplish it. The bottom line is to just do it. Make it a core value of your organization and see how your team will respond to the next big change. For example, blend your training approach to the new sales process, by balancing theory with practice and adoption, role-playing, problem solving and creating an online platform for review and reinforcement. Encourage training for all parties and make the learning simple. Too many moving parts (words and concepts) are problematic to manage.

World class athletes have coaches. Michael Jordan had a coach. Wayne Gretzky had a coach. While they may not coach the art behind the skill of the athlete, they still work hands-on to provide insight into the mechanics of the skill. This provides perspective and knowledge, as well as showing the team you are paying attention to them. For example, during implementation of the new sales process, plan for consistent and ongoing touch points and pulse checks with the team on their abilities, skills and performance.

People need and want feedback. They want to know where they stand and how they are performing. Many managers will offer feedback and all too often it is only related to what the team member can do better or improve. Feedback must have a balance of positive and corrective direction. It must also be two-way if you wish to increase its effectiveness. What managers fail to see is the base underlying need of all humans to be recognized. For example, during implementation of the new sales process, praise and recognize effort. Be sure to finish your comment with a specific behavior and an acknowledgement tailored to the personality of the team member.

Things will get in the way! What may stop you? As you think about something new on the horizon or begin planning a new way of conducting business, think about what happened last time things changed. Was it a success or did it fail miserably? If it did succeed, what contributed to the overall success? And if it failed, what were the causal points? Research has shown change (a.k.a. new standard or initiative) often ends with degrees of failure. It comparatively suggests there is on opposite ends both complete success and complete failure, but they are in the minority.

Time is perhaps the biggest. With pressure to show financial results, the tendency for most organizations is to expect the short term and anything needing time to develop is quickly pushed to the side. "Unless I can see it right now or reap benefit tomorrow, it isn't worth my time." Allow for a timely assessment; especially from goals development to deployment to auditing effectiveness. Do not change more than you (and especially your team) can absorb and execute. Create timely and consistent pulse checks throughout implementation.

Then there is Chaos. Wouldn't we all agree the word chaos carries a certain negative connotation? Managers tend to embrace an obsessive desire to control as many things as possible. So when things go awry, and mistakes are made, managers feel compelled to grab their perceived control thereby suppressing the activity of their subordinates. Chaos will be natural and inherent in any change. It doesn't matter if these subjective feelings such as fear, anxiety, doubt, and uncertainty are commonplace. Do not let your ego get in the way of the learning process. Chaos is healthy and necessary so turn it into team building and brainstorming.

Lack of support appears typically in two different ways. One, senior management designs and drives the change from the top down without any involvement by those below; causing distrust and a general feeling of flavor of the month. Two, implementation is requested but not supported by senior management; leaving supervisors feeling devalued and without power to create change. If you are in a role of leadership, request the feelings and insight from those involved in the change. Explain how the change will reinforce the vision and values of the entire organization and its cultural branding. Continuously pass information during development and make people aware of the significance of change. Create a shared vision and common direction by explaining specifically how the change will affect all parties.

Architecture is the structure of change. Ever heard this, "Why should we change that?" Also, ever tried to create a plan only to find out something came up you didn't expect? Designing a plan is not easy. While it may contain simple elements, it is made up of several parts and the most common pitfall is not thinking about what may happen. This includes variables like your team, clients and support entities. Implementing a plan or strategy is first based on identifying and using key information from all organizational stakeholders to produce results. Identify how your plan supports the vision and the objectives. Identify any obstacles and take measures of prevention. Monitor and evaluate your processes continuously throughout implementation and always look for improvements. Avoid change inflexibility and encourage imagination, innovation, inquiry and creative problem solving.

Most organizations do not successfully measure results outside of the bottom line. These quantitative numbers (i.e. total sales, gross profit, total productivity output) are the result of much greater, more dynamic causal factors (i.e. behaviors), and consequently problematic for most people to track and measure, because they do not get the correlation. Also at issue is measurement that only occurs after change has taken place without the data prior to the change taking place. Another may be, they don't pick the correct metrics to measure. If you don't currently track metrics, start. Ensure you have alignment between your targeted goals and the metrics they affect and share all goals and metrics with those being measured.

If the saying goes "change is inevitable", this must suggest not only it is probable, it is also essential. As managers, you must become fixed on how to make change do-able. From my book *What If?* I leave you with this thought – Be proactive in being reactive.

Activities

Discussion: What are your frustrations regarding change? Make a list for yourself or include this within a team meeting to brainstorm ideas.

Discussion & Exercise: Define a current goal or objective. It can be anything your company is implementing.

- Define/List your place within the goal or objective. This would be your role and list of responsibilities.

- Define/List your team's place within the goal or objective. This would be their role and list of responsibilities.

- Define/List those things which may pose as a roadblock to your success.

Discussion: Read the following statement and offer your thoughts as it applies to implementing change. *A Gallup study of nearly 5 million employees reveals that an increase in recognition and praise can lead to lower turnover, higher customer loyalty and satisfaction scores, and increases in overall productivity.*

Exercise: Consider a goal or objective, either currently in place or being planned. Using the best practices from the previous pages, begin making notes on how you can adopt change management behaviors regarding the goal.

- Communication
- Collaboration
- Support
- Acknowledgement

True success comes only when every
generation continues to develop the next
generation.

- John C. Maxwell

17

Growth

When you woke up today, what was your first thought? How about when you walked into your work environment? What about when you had your first conversation with Todd (the average performer), or Skippy (the below average performer), or perhaps Mary (the above average performer)? At what point and to what degree are you willing to give yourself to their development? What does growth mean for a team member?

As manager, the goal is to get "it" done. Is growing the team part of getting "it" done? A program of development is essential. It is the thing a person looks at to move themselves or stimulate ideas or change the status quo. It makes perfect sense, and yet some organizations just want to get the "it" done. They do not look at their team members and say "I grow the business by growing my people." They only look at moving the levers in the business, not the people and their abilities to move the levers.

The day you become a manager, you may not know what is expected to grow others. Think about this. What is necessary to be in place to grow others properly? Do they need training, coaching, what? Growth is about getting insight, direction, inspiration and feedback.

Managers have been given the responsibility to manage their business. You cannot build and sustain a strong business and culture unless everyone on your team is on the same page. This task involves using your influence to continually reinforce that commitment. The key is to think of growth, to think of how a team member moves towards making a goal happen. How can you influence someone's ability to hit targets in a way that makes them think "I am part of this and I am better as a result of it"?

Your success or failure is linked your team's abilities and performance. It must stressed this effort includes requirements like standards and expectations which need to be fulfilled every day. It also includes the variables which will challenge your decision making. This is the engine in any given day. A manager must be willing to grow a team member with all efforts necessary to accomplish that goal regardless of challenges. You must be willing to wake up and make someone else better. This ultimately makes up your commitment, your mindset to develop others.

The relationship between a manager and team member will always need to be nurtured. Growth remains poorly understood, often being targeted as forced mentoring, motivating and advising. The strategic rationale for growth may be also ignored, with growth mistakenly being presented as some kind of abstract training or coaching session. In essence, there needs to be some type of growth track or cycle for the team member to better them, period.

Well-oiled businesses have a very detailed path or life cycle for their team members. From the day they start and even up until an intended or unintended departure, there exists a series of milestones. These milestones are designed to support the growth and development of the team member.

The importance must be placed on having each step defined and having an assigned time line for each step. This allows both leadership and team members to understand and plan what happens next. The following represents a minimum table of team member life cycle milestones.

A proactive recruitment program focuses on resources providing the greatest possible return; especially recruitment referral program, networking, etc. A formalized interview process is a two to three-step process with documentation and can take up to two weeks. It must include a review of job responsibilities, requirements, conditions of employment, etc. Hiring is a one to two-day formalized process with documentation meant to review all future milestones and overall performance management. The orientation process can take up to one-week. It provides all insight and documentation into company, job and overall employment requirements.

Initial training can vary in length; from one and two-weeks up to one-month. It is constructed as a formalized training schedule with documentation. It defines structure including all methods, measurement and follow-up. Ongoing training must be provided as needed with its own detailed development track.

Consider the value of the review of the new hire process in 30 to 90-day increments with documentation. It is specifically designed to review all skills, abilities and knowledge as a first step of performance management. It represents a formalized growth and development process with documentation. It is the defined structure of coaching, performance review, and the ability for team member feedback on the organization. From six-months to one-year, some type of formalized succession process with documentation must be established to define all ongoing expectations and requirements.

In a recent human resources forum poll, 16 percent of the respondents had no performance appraisal system at all. Another 16 percent described their appraisals as based solely on supervisor opinions.

When a team member leaves an organization, exit interviews are a simple one-hour (or less) formalized process with documentation to evaluate the departing team member's overall employment feedback.

Therefore, if I work for you, what happens during my tenure? Has the organization looked at what makes an team member valuable? What does my performance suggest? Any performance management cycle must be a consistent, ongoing process helping both managers and team members to create a platform to establish clear expectations, review performance, next steps and then provide two-way feedback regarding these expectations and goals.

Any cycle must be designed to encourage open dialogue, objective data and on-going communication about performance. The following represent typical phases within a performance management cycle.

Establish every performance expectation. It is the communication of objectives and plans with targets and time lines. In effect, this allows the team to be successful. It promotes an understanding of what needs to be done, to what degree and by what time frame.

Reviewing the performance explores an evaluation of performance, identification of achievements and opportunities for improvement. It is the looking at the numbers or objective facts with a mindset to understand "what is the relationship between what one did and the result". This is cause-effect.

Coach the action plan, as well as the provision of feedback and insight into targeted expectations. It must also include the provision of direction for reinforcement and improvement. By the way, coaching must never be just one thing; it has to be many things and approached in many ways. Also consider the balance of reward and reconstruction.

Follow up is what is missed most in a performance management reality. You risk more by not following up than by the time and effort it may take to follow up. Anything and everything you do must always have some type of follow-up. For instance, coaching must have a part two. So to put it in proper perspective, this is less a step in the cycle. It is more a bridge or link back to establishing the expectations.

The performance management cycle is behaviorally-based. It starts with communication. Simply put, to perform is to know. Think about the team member and their needs whenever you position a thing (e.g., a task, goal, objective). Rate your own ability to communicate. Then consider each person communicates differently. Be sure to ask questions to clarify understanding. Don't just tell it or "shove it down someone's throat", instead inspire and influence your team's desire to do it on their own. Always put things in both the small picture (tactical) and big picture (strategic).

Everyone wants to know they are on some type of path to somewhere. It may include coaching, reviews or succession planning. This becomes important to put team members on any path of growth. Ensure all efforts are being done consistently, in an ongoing manner and with specific relevance to the team member. Always acknowledge the behavior. Nothing cements behavior more than immediate praise and recognition as well as re-constructive feedback. All acknowledgements are best served in a positive light. Make this a two-way street. Engage all learning and growth in a collaborative environment.

Documentation is both time consuming and very important. Because it is impossible to recall every little detail within a team member's life cycle, documentation provides an objective trail which supports and substantiates events, claims, and issues. Consider some type of log as a means of documenting any and all coaching and development. This effort ensures a library of reference for coaching, reviews and potential corrective action. Documentation must create a landscape so that anyone who knows nothing about the team member or situation can then have an accurate picture. It must be considered a legal document. Therefore, keep it factual and specific. It must have at a minimum the "what, why, how and to what extent". It should be secured in the team member's file within a locked filing cabinet.

No matter how you explain it, consequences have a negative vibe regardless of the context. The definition of a consequence is a result of a behavior, which implies both positive and negative. It must be clear to the team member what happens when they make a behavioral choice. Make all discussions of consequences for all performance as proactive as possible. This includes both good and poor performance. Be sure objectivity is at the heart of any review or next step. Follow through with anything you state or define. If you are not willing to follow through with it, do not say it.

Sometimes you will face performance problems requiring a more aggressive course of action like corrective action. Context will establish which progressive discipline step is most appropriate. This will help you focus on the process and not the person. Always analyze both the expectations of the business and the scope of the issue. Objectivity allows you to improve performance or maintain performance, not to punish the person. At this stage, if you have not already, document everything.

Activities

Discussion: Identify the milestones of your team member life cycle. Explore the current methodology for getting them through the cycle. Review the steps within the current performance management cycle. Clarify the current corrective action progression.

Discussion: Consider the athlete – A lot of a coach's work is not just about technique, it's about getting the athletes to raise their aspirations, to get them to achieve more than they previously thought possible. It is not about 'ra-ra' motivation, it's about providing the means to improve their performance, i.e. a tool kit for better handling sales targets and overall performance. How does this concept apply to your job as manager?

Activities

Reflection: You have a team of three. One is eager to move on and they have potential. Another is eager but lacks the overall skills necessary to move one. The other does not want to move on, but is very sensitive to the others. What do you do?

Exercise: If you could plan your own performance management cycle, what would it entail?

A good manager doesn't try to eliminate conflict; he tries to keep it from wasting the energies of his people.

– Robert Townsend

18

Conflict

This is potentially a very difficult chapter for all managers. In business, conflict is inevitable. What makes this so difficult? Having a bias, having to fit something within a policy guideline, having to believe there is only "black and white" or having to stand by your set of ethics and standards. In actuality, this is not so much a chapter on conflict as it is one about negotiation skills.

There are many ways to define or to analyze conflict. Conflict is most commonly referred to as some type of interaction between people who perceive some type of incompatibility or interference from each other. Ultimately the most important definition is the one with which you are the most closely aligned. In other words, the definition is meaningless until it matters to you. And you have to negotiate it. To manage people is to manage differences. To negotiate conflict is to respect differences.

Key to our understanding is that not all conflict is on the surface and in your face. Many times is can lie under the surface and brew and fester. This is not to presume we are always in conflict, but it is to suggest there are some commonalities in the types of conflict we find ourselves in. Managers must embrace conflict. It can be internal or external conflict. Conflict can involve people, roles (tasks) or concepts (ideas). It can be easy or incredibly complex.

Studies show when you are put into a bad mood or given negative energy 50 percent goes to everyone around you, 25 percent goes back to the source and 25 percent goes inward and later to those who are close to you. These numbers are very telling and create a perspective on how to move through conflict as a general rule. If you think about it, the goal of a manager is not to eliminate all conflict. That would be both impossible and impractical. The goal should be to help a team better navigate or negotiate it. This implies some type of process. The following represents the A.C.T. model for when you find yourself either in conflict, negotiating or managing others through conflict.

Assess the situation. Collect any pertinent facts, perspectives and resources; make them available during conversation. Begin creating relational goals to ensure your path for resolution. Be sure to investigate any serious conflict with third parties if necessary.

Communicate openly. Make it known feedback will be shared and therefore create an agreement to respect the conversation. Confirm you will not be choosing sides. Establish listening rules; one person speaks at a time. If you feel an urge to say something in immediate response, make a note. To ensure accuracy, verify your understanding by taking moments throughout the communication to give your relative understanding of the situation and the other's needs.

Target the next steps. Explore next steps collectively; even if total resolution is not possible. Brainstorm ideas to improve the relationship and situation. Always remain focused on strengthening the relationship. Not only agree and commit to a next step, but also assign a way to monitor it. Assure both parties of your faith in their ability to resolve their differences.

Remember, conflict does not have to only be a negative experience where at least one person loses. Think of a time when you were engaged in some type of conflict and the result was good. In other words, you went "ahh, no, not this" and ended with "I am so glad we got that out in the open. I feel a lot better". Conflict can have distinctive benefits.

Conflict can release tension. As tension builds during conflict, it must have a release. The key is to allow release in safe and supportive environment. Conflict can also air out issues. It allows people to share what is causing difficulties and inefficiencies.

Ultimately, conflict can strengthen relationships. As manager and leader, you are getting things done through others and that inherently means you are in a relationship. Even in the worst of times, conflict can bring people together.

Conflict stimulates change. As you work a problem or tackle an issue, focus on the creation of change and in that change look for growth opportunities. The very act of managing the conflict can cause creativity.

There are also times when conflict can cause you to re-evaluate systems, processes, procedures and the mechanisms of your organization. In that evaluation, you begin to re-define your methods, efficiencies and the better way than what you've been doing.

At the end of the day, you must choose your battles. Your conflict style, and negotiation style, will ultimately relate to the situation, your expectations for resolution and what you will bring behaviorally to the situation. Every situation will have unique nuances requiring you to change and choose the most appropriate course of action.

Sometimes you need to compete. You will be interested in getting your way or controlling the outcome. You will lack flexibility with little or no concern with the other party. This is appropriate when the maintenance of relationship is unimportant and if the decision will cost you a great deal. This is inappropriate if each party has a vested interest in success and if the issues are unimportant and immediate decision is not required.

Other times you need to collaborate. In this, you will be interested in everyone's view and will work for a collective outcome. You share control and are more focused on the issue, not the people. Primarily this works if there is an open environment. Think about if the long term relationship is an interest with time to support one another or if there is no time to dedicate to the resolution.

There are times you need to compromise. You will need to look at both parties giving something away to fix the solution. You are moderately flexible and share thoughts to empower all to a conclusion. On one side, there may be a point of non-movement or all parties are not concerned about giving something up. The flip side is an imbalance of power or the issue requires thoughtful and intense resolution.

Some conflict choices involve avoiding. You may become fearful or hope it will go away. You take away all power to address the situation and only address what you want. This is best when resolution is unlikely or if the issues can be resolved without direct interaction. This is bad if the issue is very important to you. Decision making is your responsibility or if the conflict must be resolved.

Then there is accommodation. You will give into others and allow your needs to be second to theirs. While you are flexible and willing, you may be apathetic, give away too much and not very active. Yes, you will if the importance of the issue lies more with the other party or if maintaining the relationship is key. And no, if you have very strong feelings about the issue; especially if you know you are right or if the other party is being unethical or unfair.

The healthiest individual you will find, even in the most stressful of circumstances, will be the one who has a sense of choice and control over the events in their lives. Does this mean that the unhealthiest is the one with neither? This is an issue. Stress can be at the heart of conflict. It is much more than a subjective sensation, stress is unavoidable. The workplace today is not just stressful, it is involves degrees of stress with a multitude of relative understanding, expression and ways to deal with it. As with conflict, stress can be beneficial. Though a degree of pressure can help you to perform effectively, excessive demands can reduce your productivity and make it more difficult to make important decisions.

While stress from our non-work environment can easily invade the workplace, that reality cannot be our mission. It is way too big. Therefore, our goal as manager and leader must be to be better equipped to embrace and work with it on the job even if the source does not originate at the workplace.

- Cope with your tasks. Be realistic. Do not expect too much of yourself or others. Try to be assertive, rather than passive or aggressive. Be flexible and think positive.

- Organize your time. Plan your day and make a well prioritized "to-do" list. Delegate and share responsibilities; give less important tasks to others and try less to control every situation.

- Nurture your self. Share your thoughts, hopes and fears with colleagues or superiors. Try to find humor in stressful situations. As odd as it may seem, get regular exercise and plenty of sleep and eat a healthy, balanced diet. Learn to say 'no' when appropriate. And take frequent breaks for rest and relaxation.

Activities

Reflection: How would you define your conflict management style?

- How would others define your conflict management style?

- Identify the most common kinds of conflict you face. Now list your areas of opportunity.

Discussion/Exercise: Think of a recent conflict. Now apply the ACT model; how does the outcome change?

Discussion: You have a team of people. They all have been dealing with the scope and reality of a national economic crisis. You did not create the stress and yet it is impacting the productivity of the team. What is your next step?

Discussion: The most common responses to stress are Freeze or Flight. What other responses may there also be?

Activities

A coach is someone who can give correction without causing resentment.

- John Wooden

19

Discipline

One of the hardest perceived things a manager must do is demand compliance. All too often it is confused with the need for a system of punishment. Yet if you expand your mind to include the concept of ensuring your team is staying on track, it changes the game.

Compliance is a willingness to follow a prescribed course of action. You cause that. When you create the environment whereby everyone is managed and led with the same equity, compliance is a by-product. Stop thinking compliance is about forcing people to do what you want. That is suppression and an entirely different mindset. Creating a compliant environment ensures your team will know their expected behaviors and boundaries.

The potentially difficult part of performance management is progressive discipline and it will only come into play when the team member has decided to be unwilling or non-compliant. Your goals and aspirations are always to grow and develop each team member. If they decide to be non-compliant, knowingly fall below standard or become consciously unwilling to perform a trained, coached and measured task, you have recourse.

This chapter is designed to walk you through your empowerment. It will discuss the process of checking perception to a general progressive discipline and corrective action process with tips all along the way. This chapter will explore steps within a side of management. Remember, your goal is to get your team back on track, ensure team member retention and protect the company from poor performance.

Are you struggling with what makes a disciplinary situation? Use a problem solving approach to investigate performance. A thorough investigation will ensure any potential corrective action is appropriate. The more energy spent on this step of the process, the better you are able to determine the appropriateness of the corrective action that will be taken. Managers often move too quickly to progressive steps and then later realize they contributed to the situation because of something they did or did not do. You must check what has led this team member to this situation.

The questions below allow you to objectify the situation before moving forward to disciplinary action. In other words, when in that moment of thinking "Am I going down the right path with this team member?" ask yourself these questions.

- Did I clearly define this task (issue)?

- Did I train this person?

- Did I verify understanding?

- Did I follow up to check ability?

- Did I coach appropriately to develop the ability?

- Did I objectively measure the ability?

- Have all obstacles been removed to ensure success?

If any of the answers are "No", stop and move back into development. This implies taking up where the "Yes" turned to "No", or perhaps even all the way to the beginning. If all of the answers are "Yes", you are within your rights to move progressively further into disciplinary next steps. This means you must follow a chain of events to ensure both objectivity and clarity for the team member. Your conversation and meeting must include the following at a minimum.

- Clarify the situation and issue at hand.

- Ask the team member for their perspective.

- Ensure the team member understands the situation and its serious nature.

- Ask the team member to provide their solution.

- Set a next step with targets and time line.

- Explain potential consequences for reoccurrence.

All disciplinary action or conversations require documentation. You need to be prepared to organize all the elements of the situation and record the data for review. Documentation makes up one part of your formalized process within progressive discipline, but for now we will highlight the key elements for your documentation awareness.

Always keep a professional focus. If you are at this stage, maintain a professional manner and follow the documented information. You must be consistent in your behavior as the manager. Even if you are a friend of this team member, everyone must be held to the same standard.

Assemble all the detailed facts of the situation and issue. This involves the collection of all specific actions, observations, coaching documentation, performance tracking sheets and feedback as needed regarding the expected performance. Any opinion or third party data must be verified; if it does not relate, do not use it. When you assemble your facts, be sure to place them in proper sequence from the situation in question to all that has transpired since then. This may include your observations, coaching, follow up meetings, and continued non-compliance with all associated dates regarding each. Show everything that has led you and the team member to this place.

Detail all action plans and targets of improvement. No corrective action document is complete without the two next elements. One is the specific action required on the part of the team member in their developmental improvement plan. The other highlights the clear definition of what the manager/organization is doing to support and develop the team member's behavior and over what period of time. Both must have detailed targets with associated follow-up time lines.

This is critical to your success; follow through with any and all consequences. Do not list any consequence that you will not be willing with which to follow through. If they go further, do what you said you would do. Nothing is more powerful than a manager who stands firm and nothing is more powerful than a manager who does not and the team recognizes it.

After all is discussed, have the team member read and sign all documentation. The team member must know their signature is not an admission of guilt. It confirms the conversation took place and all information was understood by the team member.

Let's be real. What is the disciplinary process? First off, your organization may very well have an established corrective action path. Choosing the right option for corrective action is the ultimate managerial question when factoring a progressive disciplinary track. The crime must always fit the punishment and there must exist a flow or path of progressive steps to follow.

Coaching is always the first step and perhaps the most time-involved. This would be the act of providing input, feedback, insight and action regarding a team member's performance. These interactions may be scheduled one-on-ones and real time conversations. Ideally all coaching conversations are documented using some type of coaching and performance log.

A verbal warning follows next. The presumption here is that you have attempted coaching and the developing of this team member, and that the involvement was progressive in nature. Now, if the team member continues with non-compliant behavior, you must escalate to a verbal warning. Verbal warnings represent a verbal conversation whereby you express the non-compliance is unacceptable and should he or she continue with this behavior it will escalate further to a written warning and ultimately termination if it continues further.

Although it is a verbal discussion, it is always a best practice to document the conversation on your corrective action document and place in team member file. Should you document, it is not necessarily mandatory for the team member to sign a verbal warning.

Written warnings and/or letters of reprimand represent the next step. As serious as this stage is, you are still not on a course to fire anyone. One, this is the "are you sure you want to continue this behavior?" step. And it also is used for more severely progressive behaviors. This step allows the team member to experience your serious regard for their employment. It may very well catch them off guard. This will be the changing point for many of your team members; they may have been uncertain how far you were willing to go.

Regardless if this represents a first or second written warning, you must fill out official corrective action document. You must also confirm all data and documentation with the team member before moving progressively forward. The manager will ensure there is clear understanding by the team member of the expected behavior.

It is advised to involve both a supervisor and HR consultant at this stage. In some cases, they may be the same person. If the supervisor or HR consultant finds call for continuance and termination is not warranted, any further step may be deferred pending further coaching, counseling and development.

If the team member is still non-compliant, suspension and/or final written warning represents the "we are not talking about this anymore. You need to decide if this if the place for you." Essentially this step entails the serious nature of the situation or issue and any continuance of non-compliant behavior will whereby result in termination. By the way, be prepared for the team member to just leave and not come back. If serious, it is highly advised that a supervisor and HR consultant be involved to ensure objectivity and accuracy. This safety measure is for the benefit of all parties.

Termination is one of the most feared steps in management. This fear can lead to the team taking advantage of a manager. It can also be feared by team members, when their manager uses the power aggressively. This step must never be a surprise to either party!

This is the easiest step. The catch is you have to have done everything in an attempt to save this individual and followed all steps with proper documentation. From the team member's perspective, if everything was done to support them, the team member is really firing themselves.

Termination is a private meeting with a short and sweet discussion. There is no second guessing or chances at this point. Be the manager and move on. "You're not having any fun. I'm not having any fun. It's time you work some place else."

Please make note that disciplinary actions can easily escalate to suspension or termination based on the serious nature of the infraction. These might include but not limited to:

- Assault (physical or verbal, to a customer or another team member)
- Violence
- Harassment
- Alcohol/drug use on company time
- Theft (products and services)
- Vandalism
- Direct Insubordination
- Intentional gross misconduct
- Job abandonment (3 consecutive shifts)

Perhaps the worst or most severe fear is not the bad news itself, but the rather the delivery of it. I find the difficulty lies in the sharing of the information in the middle than in the beginning or end.

Stay objective, collect all the data and simply say what the data supports. Know the facts and know the prescribed next steps. This is a combination of having the facts and the intent to deliver the conversation.

Be sure to note that preparation is the confidence element of the conversation. Will you have the right words and tone to deliver the message? It may be important for you to craft a list or outline of what will be said and in what order. It may also be very beneficial to consider any comments or questions which the team member may bring to the discussion. Be prepared to handle all types of reactions. You may want to role-play this with someone prior to the actual meeting. Think about the quality of your questions, like "Why do you think we are speaking right now?", "Are you willing to change your behavior?", "Are you willing to lose your job over this?"

Tone will always set the stage for the conversation. Be sure you have the right tone for the right discussion. For example, you would not be as serious in a verbal warning versus a suspension. The way in which you deliver the conversation will be determined by the type of corrective action. Communication will depend on you remaining positive, patient, specific, empathetic and concerned while listening, resolving and including all consequences.

Be sure to have all documentation available. This would include but not be limited to all logs, checklists, forms, etc. Also make the environment private. Discretion is important and shows respect for the team member. Before ending the conversation, ensure the following is detailed: their expected performance, action plan, consequences, commitment and understanding of conversation (signature).

Technically, no one has to sign anything. You may need a witness should someone refuse. So select a witness; preferably an assistant manager or manager-peer. When present, ask the team member at performance issue to confirm the conversation on this issue and the understanding of its meaning. Do not discuss specifics in presence of the witness. Ask the witness if they saw the acknowledgement. If yes, have witness sign. If no, dismiss witness, discuss again. Upon completion, repeat process. If you have no witness present for the conversation, sign the form indicating that the team member has received a copy of the corrective action document and has been told of the expected performance, the consequences and the action plan but has refused to sign. Then ask if they would initial.

Just like in coaching, all progressive discipline requires follow-up. If for no other reason, it is designed to assure follow-through and ensure accountability.

Perhaps a challenging question is how long should follow-up be scheduled? This would depend on the severity of the issue or the time involved or scope of change required. A manager must either consider their own scale (two weeks for something big versus one month for something less) or what is mandated as scale by the organization.

Follow-Up will include a review of documentation, subsequent performance results, consequential reactions and relative next steps with the team member. It will include observation, feedback and any necessary escalation. The key is to establish what the business needs in conjunction with the progressive discipline.

Something often missed is the manager's ability to celebrate wins. Managers are quick to fix others and share what they could do better, however they many times lack the ability to say, "Congratulations, you are doing much better" or "You are making progress, great job." Sometimes the mentioning of improvement is enough to affect behavior and choice.

Discipline has a bad ring to it. You perhaps heard it first when you were a child and your parent had to discipline you. You wanted to avoid it, but it still came. Perhaps you are now a parent and can use that memory to understand the principle behind it. It is used to shape behavior and keep people on track, not to just control or hurt others.

Activities

Discussion: Define the current progressive discipline process for your organization.

Discussion: Identify the most common situations you face a challenge regarding progressive discipline. Why?

Discussion/Exercise: During a progressive discipline conversation...
- A team member begins to become emotional
- Says "Fine, I quit"
- Expresses "I never knew it was that big of a deal"
- Asks "but what about all the other times everyone else did the same thing"

Reflection: What are the worst scenarios and why?

Activities

We all know what to do, but do not always do what we know.

— Something I Learned

20

Congruence

Take just a moment and reflect on the scale of what you have experienced as manager. If asked what have you learned, what would you say? If asked, how will you put this all together, what would you say? At some point, you must begin looking at how this all fits together. The true challenge will not be what you learned, discussed and problem solved up till now, it is when you face something tomorrow. The true challenge is how you will fit what you know and believe when it matters most.

The Latin *congruere* means to come together or agree. Congruence means similarity between objects or things. Congruence is a relation which implies a kind of equivalence, though not complete equivalence. What this means in management or how it specifically takes shape is ultimately the agreement between what is learned and what is applied. This will happen when something you learned or know doesn't exactly fit the context of the situation you face.

The first stop is to understand the movement from knowing to doing. What have you learned? That is the retention-side of the learning. Adoption is what you do to give the learning "legs and breath". While you contemplate how to implement and adopt behaviors and standards, the immediate question may be "how do I get it started?" or "what do I do to take what I learned and make it real for myself and my team?" This is not as easy. The key to adopting any behavior is to know what best practices will help implementation. It doesn't matter what it is you may be implementing. It can be new standards or promotions or new strategic imperatives within an organization.

Communication represents the single biggest challenge for all organizations – to communicate more effectively. However, the same challenge exists in all aspects of life; whether you are in a relationship, have children or want to explain to the sales person why you are interested in the 42-inch plasma TV.

Many of the challenges we face have been caused by the very things we have invented to make our lives easier; like emails and text messaging. It is a wonder we even know how to speak to one another. Therefore, we must look at communication as the first step in working within ourselves change to know the core. It is another to understand it.

Business has unfortunately made the relationship between employer and team member transactional. An important observation goes further to say, when nothing more is offered, nothing more is given. It would be easy to surmise these are greatly influenced and acknowledged by the manager of the team. Furthermore, the U.S. Department of Labor statistics show the number one reason people leave organizations is that they "don't feel appreciated". A Gallup study of nearly 5 million team members reveals that an increase in recognition and praise can lead to lower turnover, higher customer loyalty and satisfaction scores, and increases in overall productivity.

Congruence may be seen as the act of coming together, or of being of same mind or shape, or to be in agreement. The goal is this section is to look at congruence as a balance of self versus something else in a relative context. In other words, are you true to yourself when making decisions about what needs to be done? The heart of this section is ethics.

Ethics, or rather ethical decision making, can be a difficult thing to isolate. The reason is we try to make ethics a goal, rather than the journey. Ethics is what aids in our journey, not what we seek to find in our journey. Understanding how we respond and how we shape decisions to situations will be explored

What is business ethics? When asked the same question, John C. Maxwell, author, consultant and motivational speaker, stated, "There is no such thing as business ethics, only ethics." This section will not dispute that. It will instead challenge you to understand the choices you make and what may influence you when you make them.

- Does any decision you make in the day bother you at night?

- Have you ever questioned a decision based on who you are and what you believe?

- If what you did to accomplish a goal ended up in the company newsletter, would you feel good or bad?

- Do you find yourself rationalizing or bending the rules to meet the over-arching company mission?

Will this impact ethics, decision making or attitudes toward business goals and objectives? Not necessarily. It will be very difficult to change the current filter you use to make decisions. The better approach is to make decisions that align with business goals while staying true to yourself (congruence).

It seems a bit counter-intuitive to suggest a style for such a unique and personal aspect of your life – your ethical decision making. Considering the amount of influence one has in making decisions, there are select and targeted things to consider as you align a decision making process.

It is best to start with the environment. As manager and leader you must establish the principles and guidelines, as well as role modeling for your team. As you create this environment, be very aware of the needs and perspectives of the team. While ethics is ultimately about who you are, having some type of process in place may very well aid in how you make decisions. Think things through, imagine how they might affect others and then act. Another example is one day you were a peer and now you are their leader. Is your desire to be liked? Work on that.

Be aware of ethical conflict; especially when beliefs or engrained value systems come into conflict with one another. For example, this might be your belief of something good versus someone else's belief of something good. What you think is right (or righteous) may go against another team member's or organization's perspective.

Action is the ultimate test. And with it come creativity, awareness, accountability and learning. Ethics does not just precede a decision; it is present at the "beginning, during and after". Don't expect everything to be absolutely perfect. It is about the best choice given the situation. Sometimes it is not that you are flawed, the situation and its alternatives are what is flawed.

The expression of your ethics, values, beliefs and moral philosophy come into the situations you face in life. The goal will always be to explore how your character takes shape in those situations while managing and leading others. Perhaps more importantly, how will your authenticity take shape? Your belief could be a bias that is not in alignment with what you think is the right decision. While ethics is ultimately about who you are, having some type of process in place may very well aid in how you make decisions.

What drives you? What is your passion? Many times managers know their current position is not where they want to be a year from now. They are actively (or inactively) looking for the thing they truly want to do. What will drive your decisions while you are where you are now? If you have identified your passion, and allowed it to take hold in your life, you have to share it. You must share it for free and with no conditions. Make your passion contagious. Find ways every day to allow your "passion walk and talk" help you discern and decide courses of action in management.

Will you stay on path? Management is a series of "what do I do now?" moments. Don't expect everything to be absolutely perfect. Evaluate the situation. Determine the black, white and shades of grey. Sometimes there is no right, just the least wrong. Staying congruent is about making a decision as the best choice given the situation. Be authentic.

Activities

Reflection: Read and reflect upon the following statement by John C. Maxwell, author, consultant and motivational speaker, "There is no such thing as business ethics, only ethics." What does that mean?

Reflection: If you ever face a decision which troubles you or you feel like you need to talk it out, contact a close peer or friend and brainstorm all aspects of what is troubling you.

Discussion: Is there such a thing as 'ethically bending' the rules when managing and leading your team. What are they and why?

Reflection: Identify personal characteristics you formed from each select "life categories":

FAMILY | SCHOOL | WORK | RELATIONSHIP | WORLD

Reflection: Read and reflect upon the following quote: "For where your treasure is, there will your heart be also."

Conclusion

So what now? It depends. Just like the elements in the Kirkpatrick theory associated with evaluating training, my job was to create a reaction. The learning is your responsibility, or rather what you learned you now own. As far as the behavior element, my hope is that I gave you some context, ideas and tips to construct within yourself and team. The results will come later, if you stick with it, remain diligent and measure your performance.

As you finish this book, you must decide what happens now. Maybe it is a meeting with your team about a topic. Maybe it will be a new process due to one of the ideas shared. Or maybe it will be a new way to look at the business or your job as manager. Whatever the next step, it will be very important for you to decide, plan, implement and live it every day. The hardest part will be two to three weeks from now – trust me. Your next step is right now, what is it?

I will sometimes have clients ask what is it I actually do or provide. Take this book. Every chapter highlights an aspect of management. Each chapter represents a part of my library of topics (in addition to some others). Each chapter can be made into its own course or part of one. As for the delivery, that would be up to the organization. It could be on-site facilitation, curriculum design, workshops, podcasts, webinars or an addition to existing course content.

I bring this up because what you learn in life must not be static. It must move. It must have legs and a heartbeat. I find this to be a common area either missed by a client or needing further support. If you are an owner, share these ideas. If you are a general manager or senior supervisor, drive these ideas. If you are a manager and leader of a team, live these ideas. To all, you need to first establish your own development before developing others. So, to each of you, may you grow, develop, flourish and yield good fruit.

About the Author

Kurt Reinhart is passionate about working with learners all over North America. He has been blessed to continue working with businesses as a trainer-consultant and is continuing to grow and evolve Create Training & Consulting. It is an exciting time with new things taking shape. He still resides in Fort Collins, Colorado with his beautiful wife and two daughters. Also, he excited his son is back from Afghanistan and lives with his new wife in Hawaii.